eckie × Leckie
otland's leading educational publishers

SNAP REVISION POETRY BY NORMAN MACCAIG

SNAP REVISION

POETRY BY NORMAN MACCAIG

For National 5 and Higher English

REVISE
FOR YOUR
SQA EXAMS

David Cockburn

Published by Collins
An imprint of HarperCollinsPublishers
1 London Bridge Street,
London, SE1 9GF

© HarperCollinsPublishers Limited 2018

9780008306670

First published 2018

10 9 8 7 6 5 4 3 2 1

British Library Cataloguing in Publication Data.

A CIP record of this book is available from the British Library.

Printed in United Kingdom.

Commissioning editor: Gillian Bowman
Managing editor: Craig Balfour
Author: David Cockburn
Proofreader: Jess White
Copy editor: Louise Robb
Project manager: Project One Publishing Solutions, Scotland
Typesetting: Jouve
Cover designers: Kneath Associates and Sarah Duxbury
Production: Natalia Rebow

ACKNOWLEDGEMENTS

The author and publisher are grateful to the copyright holders for permission to use quoted materials.

'Assisi', 'Aunt Julia', 'Basking Shark', 'Brooklyn Cop', 'Hotel Room, 12th Floor', 'Visiting Hour' by Norman MacCaig, reproduced by permission of Birlinn Ltd. Reproduced with permission of the Licensor through PLSclear.

From the author:
I am most grateful to Peter Doughty, ex-Principal Examiner, OCR A-level English literature, for his enlightening knowledge and inspiring understanding of MacCaig's poetry. I am also indebted to Alison Campbell, whose intelligent grasp of MacCaig's poetry and biography stems from tutorials with the poet at Stirling University. I should also like to pay tribute to Leckie and Leckie's highly talented team, whose support and consideration goes beyond expectation. And I should like to thank Kevin Cockburn without whose endless encouragement and patience this book would never have been written.

Contents

Poetry
Introduction   4

Poems
Assisi   6
Aunt Julia   10
Basking Shark   14
Brooklyn Cop   18
Hotel Room, 12th Floor   22
Visiting Hour   26

Themes
Common Themes   30
Isolation 1   32
Isolation 2   34
Nature   36
Dark Side of Human Nature   38

Techniques
Common Techniques   40
Sound Effects   42
Enjambement   44
Imagery: Comparison   46
Imagery: Representation and Contrast   48
Rhythm and Sentence Structure   50

The Exam
Preparing for the Exam   52
National 5 Exam-Style Questions   56
Higher Exam-Style Questions   62
Practice Exam   70

Glossary   72

Answers   74

This book will help you revise everything you need to know about the poetry of Norman MacCaig and the exam. You can either read it through or turn to the sections relevant to you when you revise.

This book will help you with all the stages of revision. It provides:

- a detailed analysis of all six poems; see pages 6–29
- an examination of MacCaig's themes and/or ways in which the speaker is presented; see pages 30–39
- an analysis of MacCaig's techniques by which those themes and/or the speaker have been portrayed or conveyed; see pages 40–51
- help with exam preparation, including exam-style questions with comments and possible answers, showing how marks would be allocated; see pages 52–69
- mock exam questions to provide practice; see pages 70–71
- a glossary of useful terms – handy for a quick revision check; see pages 72–73
- possible answers to all questions; see pages 74–78.

This book is aimed at students taking National 5 and at those taking Higher. All of the material is relevant to both courses except course-specific details that are denoted either N5 or H . Use these icons to guide you to sections appropriate to your course.

Approach to Norman MacCaig's poetry

MacCaig's life

Norman Alexander MacCaig was born in 1910 in Edinburgh. His mother was from Scalpay on Harris and was a great influence on both him and his poetry. Although he was brought up in Edinburgh, his Hebridean background, along with its Gaelic language and culture, was an influence on him throughout his life. His visits to his aunt in Luskentyre on West Harris, his mother's family generally and his own retreat at Assynt in Sutherland were huge influences on his poetry. He attended the Royal High School in Edinburgh, and later studied Classics at Edinburgh University. He became a teacher as well as a poet, and in 1970 was a lecturer in poetry at Stirling University.

MacCaig's poetry

One of the most fascinating and interesting aspects of MacCaig's poetry is his ability to make the ordinary seem extraordinary, the mundane appear exotic. His poetry can open our eyes, allowing us to see things in a different light, or from a new perspective. In many ways, MacCaig challenges our received ideas: that is, those ideas we have absorbed uncritically and unquestioningly from our parents, our peer group and the culture around us. In some poems he reconfirms our experiences, such as in *Visiting Hour*, while in others he reveals a darkness underlying human nature, as can be seen in *Brooklyn Cop* and *Hotel Room, 12th Floor*.

Themes

The theme of a poem is what you think the poem is about: relationships, love of someone close, unrequited love, isolation, rejection, loneliness, joy, greed, death, discovery, revenge, doubt, regret, hypocrisy – the list is endless. It is important to realise that a poem is, of course, about itself in the particular theme or narrative that it expresses, but equally the theme, narrative or character presentation has, in addition, a universal significance. The poem is ultimately making a comment on human nature, reflecting on our human condition; the poem is true in itself, but also universally true.

MacCaig's poems cover a multiplicity of themes and each poem covers more than one theme. Rather than deal with individual themes, it is more useful to deal with general ones that overlap his poems – themes such as loss, suffering, relationships, isolation and nature. In all his poems, MacCaig also explores the darker side of human nature, and yet he is able to reveal the universal significance of particular experiences, such that all his poems resonate with the wider audience.

In *Basking Shark*, for example, MacCaig does not just relate the experience of accidentally coming across a basking shark while he is at sea, he explores themes of the relationship between animals and human beings, and about how we have become so distanced from nature by our urban habitats that we have become the monsters. The poem gives details about the encounter, stating how, to begin with, the speaker saw the shark as huge and unintelligent, but as he develops his ideas he sees its grace and beauty. The poem makes clear that we have no right to feel superior to what we regard as lower creatures.

MacCaig also presents places and people in some of his poems: for example, he presents his aunt in *Aunt Julia* (page 10), the dwarf and St Francis in *Assisi* (page 6), and the speaker in *Visiting Hour* (page 26). He always has a narrator (referred to here as the speaker):

- the poem is in the first person
- a speaker addresses the reader or simply reveals his thinking
- the speaker uses language and rhythms that are close to everyday speech to give the reader access to the poetry.

Textual analysis

In your approach to the MacCaig poems, it is important that you keep in mind that the Scottish Text question is an exercise in textual analysis. At both N5 and Higher, in your response to the questions, you need to be able to refer to relevant parts of the text and then analyse your reference appropriately.

Textual analysis differs from RUAE (Reading for Understanding, Analysis and Evaluation, that is, close reading) in that it almost always involves the analysis of the writer's technique; though, of course, the RUAE paper can also ask about technique.

With all six of Norman MacCaig's poems, you need to know:

- the themes and issues explored or conveyed by each of the poems you are studying
- the various language techniques by which the themes are conveyed.

Language techniques

In N5 and in Higher, questions will invite you to refer to language techniques. As with RUAE, the term 'language' covers sentence structure, **word choice, imagery, contrast** and **tone**. But you are studying poetry, therefore you must know about structural techniques such as verse structure, **rhyme** (where appropriate), **rhythm**, sentence structure, **enjambement** and contrast. You also need to be clear as to what is meant by 'imagery': that is, techniques such as **metaphor** (including **simile** and **personification**), **oxymoron**, as well as **synecdoche** and **transferred epithet**. There are also sound techniques that you should know, such as **alliteration, assonance** and **onomatopoeia**.

Each of these terms is defined in the Glossary of useful terms on pages 72–73.

You need to have studied the poems thoroughly and know them well. You could record them on your phone so that you can listen to them as often as possible. The N5 8-mark and the Higher 10-mark questions demand that you refer to poems other than the printed one, so you must be able to quote from other poems relevant to the question.

The dwarf with his hands on backwards
sat, slumped like a half-filled sack   **A**
on tiny twisted legs from which
sawdust might run,
5 outside the three tiers of churches built
in honour of St Francis, brother
of the poor, talker with birds, over whom   **B**
he had the advantage
of not being dead yet.

10 A priest explained
how clever it was of Giotto   **C**
to make his frescoes tell stories
that would reveal to the illiterate the goodness
of God and the suffering
15 of His Son. I understood
the explanation and   **D**
the cleverness.

A rush of tourists, clucking contentedly,
fluttered after him as he scattered   **E**
20 the grain of the Word. It was they who had passed
the ruined temple outside, whose eyes   **F**
wept pus, whose back was higher
than his head, whose lopsided mouth   **G**
said Grazie in a voice as sweet
25 as a child's when she speaks to her mother
or a bird's when it spoke
to St Francis.

Context

On a visit to the Basilica of St Francis of Assisi, MacCaig was struck by the ironic gap between St Francis's work with the poor and the church, itself built in his honour, now more famous as a tourist attraction and architectural landmark than as a monument to St Francis himself. St Francis was a 12th-century priest; despite being rich, he lived as a beggar in Rome in order to understand the difficulties of being poor.

Themes

The poem deals with poverty, disability, isolation, loss, suffering, hypocrisy and apathy.

Structure

The poem uses **first-person narration** in three verse paragraphs, each portraying different scenes, along with the speaker's observations and reflections of his disturbing visit to the Basilica of St Francis. Verse 1 is one sentence, while verses 2 and 3 comprise two sentences each. The sentence structure overtakes the line structure, with the sentences 'spilling over' from one line to the next, a device known as **enjambement**.

Annotations

A Lines 1–4: highlight the defects and suffering of the dwarf. The image 'hands on backwards' conveys the extent of his appalling deformities, while the **simile** 'half-filled sack' not only recalls the hessian that used to be worn by monks, but also suggests by 'half-filled' and 'slumped' that he cannot support himself, that he is not quite human; 'twisted legs from which / sawdust might run' creates the impression of his legs being wooden with sawdust pouring from them – a shocking image that makes it clear he has great difficulty in sitting. The alliteration of the unpleasant **sibilant** and 't' sounds adds to the shock of the images.

The verse uses **enjambement**, where the sentences 'spill over' from one line to the next; the effect of this is to create shock at the beginning of the spilled-over line. For example, in line 4 the word 'sawdust' comes as a shock at the beginning of that line.

Annotations (continued)

B Lines 5–9: form a **contrast** between the ugliness of the dwarf's situation and the beauty of the 'three tiers of churches': the **irony** lies in the absurdity of an architecturally stunning church built at great expense, 'in honour' of a priest who devoted his life to the poor, especially since one of those he would have helped is begging outside the basilica. The irony takes on a darker tone in the final two lines of the verse, where the speaker makes clear that the only advantage that the dwarf has over St Francis is that he is still alive, though the final word 'yet' implies that it might not be for long.

C Lines 10–15: the scene shifts to the priest explaining the point about **Giotto's frescoes**, though he is more interested in Giotto's artistic skills than in the Biblical message that Giotto was revealing to the illiterate. Here the speaker uses an angrily **sarcastic tone** as he highlights the superiority the priest feels while not noticing the dwarf, showing that the church is out of touch with the very people it is supposed to help.

D Lines 15–17: the tone shifts again in the final three lines of the verse as the speaker scathingly attacks the priest's knowledge. Because the priest is demonstrating his pride in his ability to explain the frescoes, the speaker reviles him by the sarcastic tone of 'cleverness' – he doesn't actually mean that the man is clever, rather he means the opposite: that the priest is superficial and lacking in humanity.

E Lines 18–20: an extended **metaphor** is used, comparing the tourists to hens. The tourists are stupid in submissively following the priest, incapable of thinking for themselves. The metaphorical use of 'fluttered' suggests their indecisiveness and expressionless stupidity. As the tourists go pecking after the 'grain of the Word', the implication is that people just accept the teaching of the Church unthinkingly and uncritically, but there's a deeper irony – 'grain' is a food image, and while it is being scattered for the tourists, food is denied to the dwarf.

F Lines 20–22: the **rhythm** (weak/weak/strong) of 'It was **they** who had **passed**' stresses the word 'they', thus clarifying that the speaker emphatically dissociates himself from the tourists who ignore the 'ruined temple outside', a metaphor that compares the dwarf to a temple, a building for worship, to be respected and cherished, yet it is 'ruined', neglected, dilapidated. The wording 'ruined temple' is a reference to *Corinthians* 3:16: 'your body is a temple of the Holy Spirit who is in you' – the tourists ignore the human 'ruined temple' in favour of the grandiose 'three tiers of churches' erected to the saint who *chose* to live as a beggar in spite of his position of social advantage, while the dwarf has no choice in his lifestyle, and the only 'advantage' is that of still being alive. However, it is a life of disability, invisibility, multi-layered suffering and poverty. The enjambement (lines 21–22) isolates the words 'wept pus' at the beginning of line 22, thereby shocking the reader by the repulsive nature of the image.

G Lines 20–27: by his use of the climactic **list** as well as the **anaphora** (repetition) – 'who', 'whose', 'whose' – the speaker contrasts the sheer suffering and ugly appearance of the dwarf, whose 'eyes / wept pus', whose back is 'higher / than his head', and who has 'lopsided mouth'. The speaker uses contrast, along with the use of the list and anaphora, to compare once again the physical ugliness and disgusting appearance of the dwarf to St Francis in the first verse and to the child in the lines that follow. The speaker uses the list of the dwarf's repulsive features to stress how hideous he looks as well as anaphora of the **relative pronoun** 'whose' (making clear to whom these features belong). The use of enjambement then forces 'said Grazie in a voice as sweet' onto the next line, drawing attention to the way the dwarf's outward appearance contrasts with his kindness, politeness and inner beauty. The comparison with a child evokes our sympathy and makes us aware of his anguish and helplessness. The final two lines refer back to St Francis, who was so kind that birds spoke to him.

Question
Look at lines 1–4.
By referring to two examples of language, explain/analyse how the poet engages our sympathy for the dwarf.   4

Aunt Julia spoke Gaelic
very loud and very fast.   **A**
I could not answer her —
I could not understand her.   **B**

5   She wore men's boots   **C**
when she wore any.
— I can see her strong foot,
stained with peat,
paddling with the treadle of the spinningwheel
10   while her right hand drew yarn   **D**
marvellously out of the air.

Hers was the only house
where I've lain at night   **E**
in the absolute darkness
15   of a box bed, listening to
crickets being friendly.

She was buckets
and water flouncing into them.   **F**
She was winds pouring wetly
20   round house-ends.
She was brown eggs, black skirts   **G**
and a keeper of threepenny bits
in a teapot.

Aunt Julia spoke Gaelic   **H**
25   very loud and very fast.
By the time I had learned
a little, she lay   **I**
silenced in the absolute black
of a sandy grave
30   at Luskentyre. But I hear her still, welcoming me
with a seagull's voice   **J**
across a hundred yards
of peatscrapes and lazybeds
and getting angry, getting angry
35   with so many questions   **K**
unanswered.

Context

Aunt Julia is about MacCaig's relationship with his Gaelic-speaking aunt, who lived on the Isle of Harris, where his mother was from. He retained family links with Harris in the Outer Hebrides. Like his aunt (and unlike MacCaig), his mother could also speak Gaelic. Though born in Edinburgh, MacCaig divided his time between that city and Assynt, just north of Ullapool.

Themes

Obviously, the poem is about the loss and death of his aunt as well as lack of communication. The poem also deals with relationships and the place of nature in life. But as with all MacCaig's poetry, think beyond the simplicity of his language – the poem explores the gap between modern Scotland and the culture and heritage of island life in a previous era.

Structure

Aunt Julia uses **first-person narration**, using **free verse** in a five-verse structure: verses 1–4 are narrated by the speaker as a boy, the final verse as an adult. The use of first person and free verse create for the reader the speaker's impressions and reminiscences of his aunt, as a boy and later as a man. The use of first person also allows for reflection on the speaker's experiences.

Annotations

A Lines 1–2: the use of **repetition** – 'very' – highlights the speaker's impression of his aunt. The **adjective** intensifies the way in which Aunt Julia is highly vocal and strident (shrill). The barrier to his understanding is that she speaks too quickly, in addition to speaking in a language he didn't understand.

B Lines 3–4: the use of repetition – 'I could not' – highlights his frustration at not being able to communicate. He is unable to answer her questions because she spoke in Gaelic, which also indicates to the reader the isolation of the setting.

Annotations (continued)

C Lines 5–8: her wearing 'men's boots' reflects her lifestyle, her hard existence, her self-sufficiency, as well as, perhaps, her masculinity.

D Lines 9–11: the 'paddling' of her 'spinningwheel' is a **contrasting** image, suggesting her more feminine, domestic side, as well as indicating traditional island crafts; 'marvellously' indicates the boy's fascination with what appears magic to him.

E Lines 12–16: the whole verse evokes the remoteness in time and place of the setting. The expression 'only house' suggests that his aunt's house was unique, and that he felt completely safe there, while 'absolute darkness' is the physical, but temporary, darkness of a place with no street lights, and 'box bed' – an old-fashioned bed boxed into the living room – suggests the lack of modern comfortable furniture. The anthropomorphism (ascribing human characteristics to animals) – 'crickets being friendly' – suggests that it is the speaker who is happy, enjoying the closeness with nature.

F Lines 17–20: the **synecdoche** – 'buckets' and 'water flouncing into them' – represents her hard life: there is no running water, she has to collect it. The expressions 'winds pouring wetly / round house-ends' represent the harsh conditions created by the weather and how she is part of the force of nature.

G Lines 17–23: the use of synecdoche – the 'brown eggs', 'black skirts' and the 'keeper of threepenny bits' (old pre-decimal money, worth about 14p in today's money) – helps to represent her routine, traditional and frugal existence. The whole verse uses **anaphora** – repetition of 'She was' – which heads a list cumulatively showing the intensity of her harsh life, and at the same time showing how she represents a culture, a heritage and a way of life now gone.

H Lines 24–25: the repetition of the first two lines of the poem – reinforcing the speaker's impression of Aunt Julia's strong, vibrant voice in a language he doesn't understand – further intensifies his frustration at not being able to communicate with her. The reference is structural, suggesting the circular nature of the experience – he has gone full circle, from child to adult.

I Lines 26–29: the perspective changes to the speaker as an adult. He knows 'a little' Gaelic, but now Aunt Julia is dead. The use of **enjambement** causes the word 'silenced' to be highlighted by its position at the beginning of line 28, reinforcing the contrast with her 'loud and very fast' voice when she was alive. Further contrast is found in the 'absolute black / of a sandy grave' with the quite different 'absolute darkness' of his box bed (lines 14–15). The word 'black' **connotes** the finality of death – the darkness of death isn't temporary, unlike the darkness of his box bed.

J Lines 30–33: the **tense** switches to the present, showing how the speaker is almost defying her death – 'I hear her still'. Her loudness is again accentuated by the **metaphor** – 'seagull's voice' – which suggests her links to rural Scotland and its seas. The 'hundred yards' draws attention to just how far her voice will carry, even in his imaginings. The term 'peatscrapes' refers to areas of peat, native to the Highlands, and 'lazybeds' refers to ridging earth for growing potatoes.

K Lines 34–36: through her voice in his imagination, the repetition of 'getting angry, getting angry' suggests that the frustration is both hers and his: as a boy he couldn't answer her questions because of the language barrier, now those unanswered questions will remain 'unanswered' (note the word is the final line of the poem) because of the barrier of death. Perhaps there is more to it: the younger generation often fails to ask the older generation (grandparents who are still alive) significant questions about their experiences of the past and also fails to ask about the wider, enduring questions about the nature of life. Is his anger about his recognition that an entire way of life may disappear permanently, like Aunt Julia herself? The ending is a particular comment but has universal significance.

> ## Question
>
> Look at lines 5–11.
>
> By referring to two examples of language, explain/analyse how MacCaig presents the speaker as a young boy. **4**

Basking Shark

To stub an oar on a rock where none should be,
To have it rise with a slounge out of the sea **A**
Is a thing that happened once (too often) to me.

But not too often – though enough. I count as gain **B**
5   That once I met, on a sea tin-tacked with rain, **C**
That roomsized monster with a matchbox brain. **D**

He displaced more than water. He shoggled me **E**
Centuries back – this decadent townee **F**
Shook on a wrong branch of his family tree. **G**

10   Swish up the dirt and, when it settles, a spring **H**
Is all the clearer. I saw me, in one fling,
Emerging from the slime of everything. **I**

So who's the monster? The thought made me grow pale **J**
For twenty seconds while, sail after sail,
15   The tall fin slid away and then the tail. **K**

Context

Alone, in a rowing boat, the speaker has unexpectedly encountered a basking shark, an experience that, at first, worried and shook him. These animals, relatively common on the west coast of Scotland, are enormous, some 30 feet (9 metres) long and, though not dangerous, would scare anyone disturbing one. The experience of meeting the shark prompted this poem.

Themes

MacCaig recognises that all animals arise from the same primordial source and goes on to question our development into urban creatures who are now far removed from nature; he is questioning the place of humans, postulating that we are in no position to feel superior to other animals. We need to question our place in nature. The ordinary encounter takes on extraordinary significance.

Structure

The poem is unusually structured using five 3-line verses, with a **rhyme scheme** of *a a a b b b ...*, unusual for MacCaig, creating a tight structure, capturing the intensity of the experience and of the speaker's thought processes. MacCaig's poetry typically uses **free verse**, where he can manipulate line structure, but here the regularity of **rhyme** and **rhythm** replicates the rhythm of the gentle swelling of waves and the movement of the shark.

Annotations

A Lines 1–3: the structure of repeating (**anaphora**) **infinitives** at the beginning of lines 1 and 2 captures the reader's attention, makes us wonder what is happening and thereby creates **tension**; the word 'stub' suggests he has hit something solid, like a rock, scaring and confusing him. The **onomatopoeic** 'slounge' creates the impression of the shark displacing the water and rising slowly out of it. Line 3 makes clear that the speaker is frightened – the word 'thing' means that he can't identify the experience, but the **parenthetical** '(too often)' is an attempt to lighten the mood somewhat.

Annotations (continued)

B Line 4: the sentence in the next verse begins with 'But', which suggests a change in the speaker's thinking, almost a contradiction – 'not too often' – the encounter wasn't *that* upsetting, but the dash signals that he doesn't want to repeat the experience. The word 'gain' informs the reader that there was something beneficial about the experience.

C Line 5: the **metaphor** 'tin-tacked with rain' is particularly effective: a tin-tack is a drawing pin, and if you can imagine it upside down (the flat bit of the drawing pin downwards), then you get a mental picture of each raindrop – the pin of the drawing pin – hitting the sea causing a tiny circular wave – the flat bit – on the surface of the sea, suggesting that the sea is calm enough to see – and hear – the raindrops hit it. The **alliteration** of the 't' captures the sound of the rain hitting the calm sea.

D Line 6: the other metaphors – 'roomsized monster' and 'matchbox brain' – also concern shape: we associate rooms with being large (certainly larger than a basking shark), suggesting the sheer size and shape of the animal, but it is also effective because it is an exaggeration – a **hyperbole** (another kind of comparison). The image's light-hearted **tone** is reinforced by the **alliteration** of the 'm' and 'b' in 'matchbox brain', comparing minute size (a matchbox isn't big) with the animal's brain, suggesting not only its diminutive capacity but its primordiality (primitive species). The word 'monster' conveys the speaker's feelings of superiority – the shark is primitive in comparison.

E Line 7: there is another change in the speaker's thinking: the shark 'displaced more than water', **literally** in that the shark's bulk shifted a volume of water, but metaphorically in that the shark's presence shifted the speaker's thinking. The Scots word 'shoggled' conjures an unsteady, wobbly lurch in the speaker's thinking back to the origins of life.

F Line 8: the central idea of the poem occurs with 'decadent townee': here the speaker suggests that, to their detriment, townspeople have become dissociated from nature, that their lives are self-indulgent and hedonistic (their lives devoted to enjoyment), a long way from 'Centuries back' when their lives were about survival.

G Line 9: additionally, 'Shook on a wrong branch of his family tree' makes clear that he thinks that, to their detriment, 'decadent townee[s]' may have had a common ancestor 'Centuries back' but have now ended up on the 'wrong branch' of the tree of life – where all animals belong – an implied criticism that humans have developed in the wrong direction. The word 'shook' suggests the position on the tree is unsteady, precarious.

H Line 10: the onomatopoeic 'Swish' refers to the sudden, rapid movement of water that stirs up sediment which, once settled, allows us to see the spring of water. But it is also metaphoric – the encounter with the shark stirs up in his mind sediment or confusion, which, once settled, clarifies his thinking.

I Lines 11–12: he realises in one leap that all life originated from 'the slime of everything', the primordial soup (where in theory life began). The basking shark and humans stem from the same original source.

J Lines 13–14: then he poses the enormous philosophical question – 'So who's the monster?' – as he reflects on the nature of human beings, a thought that disturbs and shocks him for 'twenty seconds'. Note the use of **contrast**: the realisation of who is the monster takes him only twenty seconds after having been thrown back twenty centuries.

K Lines 14–15: the **assonance** of the long vowel sounds – 'pale', 'sail after sail' and 'tail', along with the **repetition** of 'sail' – captures the elegance and gracefulness of the shark as it moves away from the speaker. Moreover, the change in rhythm in the last verse slows the pace of the poem, making it more reflective, and the sheer length of the last sentence, along with the internal rhymes, suggests the enormous length of the shark. The last phrase 'and then the tail' further suggests the slowness of the shark's movement, taking us back to the shark of the title.

> ### Question
>
> How effective do you find the last verse as a conclusion to the poem?　　2

Brooklyn Cop

Built like a gorilla but less timid, **A**
thick-fleshed, steak-coloured, with two
hieroglyphs in his face that mean **B**
trouble, he walks the sidewalk and the
5 thin tissue over violence. This morning,
when he said, "See you, babe" to his wife, **C**
he hoped it, he truly hoped it.
He is a gorilla **D**
to whom "Hiya, honey" is no cliché.

10 Should the tissue tear, should he plunge through
into violence, what clubbings, what **E**
gunshots between Phoebe's Whamburger
and Louie's Place.

Who would be him, gorilla with a nightstick,
15 whose home is a place **F**
he might, this time, never get back to?

And who would be who have to be **G**
his victims?

Context

In the 1960s, during his visit to New York, a city notorious then for its violence and corruption, MacCaig wrote *Brooklyn Cop* and *Hotel Room, 12th Floor*. He was struck by the constant blare of police car and ambulance sirens, and by the threatening, terrifying appearance of a New York policeman. Brooklyn was a particularly tough and violent part of New York; Phoebe's Whamburger and Louie's Place were real places.

Themes

The poem presents a convincing character, and deals with isolation, fear, suffering, violence, human nature, good and evil.

Structure

Unlike his other poems, *Brooklyn Cop* is in the **third person**, where the speaker, **persona** or narrator is an onlooker. There are four verses and the use of the present **tense** gives the poem an immediacy, as though we are present along with the speaker. The first verse deals with the cop's rather comic-book appearance and details the relationship with his wife. The second verse explores the street violence he faces. In the third verse, the fragility of civilised society is explored and the final verse reflects on the violence of which the cop himself is capable.

Annotations

 A Lines 1–2: the poem begins with a **clichéd simile**, a **stereotype**: the cop is compared to a gorilla, which signifies his enormous size and brutal strength, though the phrase 'but less timid' reinvigorates the cliché, as it humorously suggests that the cop is even more vicious. The **compound adjectives** 'thick-fleshed' and 'steak-coloured' are **metaphors** portraying the cop's face as animal-like and tough; his features are dark – both physically and emotionally.

Annotations (continued)

B Lines 3–5: a hieroglyph is a form of writing associated with Ancient Egypt, consisting of representative pictures that aren't always easy to read. Here, MacCaig is using it as a **symbol** that can be 'read' as facial disfigurement and, at the same time, a sign that he can be 'trouble'; the **enjambement** forces the word 'trouble' onto the beginning of the next line, thereby highlighting it; the **metaphor** 'tissue' creates a contrast between the tough cop and the delicacy of tissue; 'he walks the sidewalk' is physical and hard, while in the next line 'thin tissue over violence' is metaphorical, suggesting that a civilised society (represented by the 'sidewalk)' can so easily tear apart (represented by 'tissue') and descend into violence.

C Lines 6–7: the scene shifts to his home, where he greets his wife with the stereotypical '"See you, babe"', devoid really of any emotional meaning – it's routine, expressionless – but the **repetition** of 'he hoped it, he truly hoped it' makes clear his underlying vulnerability that he hides from his wife.

D Lines 8–9: the next image moves from the simile in line 1 to the metaphor in line 8, highlighted by being in a line by itself – 'He is a gorilla'. The metaphor makes the comparison more certain, hardening the brutal, tough, heartless image of the cop – at home he is vulnerable, but outside he appears hard and invincible. Nonetheless, the comment that '"Hiya, honey" is no cliché' suddenly and surprisingly contrasts the earlier '"See you, babe"' and makes us abruptly aware of how exposed to danger he is.

E Lines 10–13: these lines reveal the deadly street violence he faces: the repetition of 'should' in 'should the tissue tear, should he plunge', with the **alliteration** of the 't' sound and the **kinetic images** (images involving movement) of 'tear' and 'plunge', all combine to create the idea of destruction, resulting in falling uncontrollably from a great height. The repetition of 'what' accentuates cumulatively the dangers of 'clubbings' and 'gunshots', all heightened by **assonance** (the ugliness of the **guttural** 'u' sound), showing just how violent the streets of New York were at that time. The names 'Phoebe's Whamburger' – the **onomatopoeia** of 'Whamburger' making the place sound so perilously violent – and 'Louie's Place', which sounds so seedy, are real place names from that time, and therefore even more chilling.

F Lines 14–16: the **penultimate** verse is structured as a **rhetorical question** – that is, one that implies its own answer. The question engages our sympathy for the cop – we would not want to be him – and the insertion of the **parenthetical** 'this time' furthers our sympathy as we understand that he might not make it back to the safety of home. The repetition of the gorilla metaphor – now he is a 'gorilla with a nightstick' (truncheon) – nevertheless reminds us that he is strong but savage, unemotional, aggressive and ready to attack, with a weapon no less. There is a **contrast** between his dangerous job as a cop and the safety of his own home.

G Lines 17–18: the last sentence begins with an 'And', the effect of which is to isolate and highlight the final point about to be made. It is also another rhetorical question, but structured in a way that causes a double-take. The criminals are seen as 'his victims', causing the reader to pause to absorb the point. The clause 'who have to be his victims' is the **complement** of the verb 'would be' (the verb 'to be' takes a complement, agreeing in number and case with the subject) – and then we realise that the cop can be as violent as the criminals. He becomes a symbol for so many people, capable of both good and evil. Despite being a protector of law and order, he is capable of being evil.

Question

Look at lines 10–16.

By referring to at least two examples of language, show how MacCaig creates sympathy for the cop.

4

This morning I watched from here
a helicopter skirting like a damaged insect
the Empire State Building, that   **A**
jumbo size dentist's drill, and landing
5   on the roof of the PanAm skyscraper.
But now Midnight has come in
from foreign places. Its uncivilised darkness   **B**
is shot at by a million lit windows, all
ups and acrosses.

10   But midnight is not   **C**
so easily defeated. I lie in bed, between
a radio and a television set, and hear   **D**
the wildest of warwhoops continually ululating through
the glittering canyons and gulches –
15   police cars and ambulances racing   **E**
to broken bones, the harsh screaming
from coldwater flats, the blood   **F**
glazed on the sidewalks.

The frontier is never
20   somewhere else. And no stockades   **G**
can keep the midnight out.

Context

MacCaig wrote this poem in the late 1960s, when the Empire State Building and PanAm headquarters were regarded as measures of the USA's power, wealth and international influence. PanAm airline was global, a measure of America's world domination until its collapse in 1991. In the title, *Hotel Room* indicates a visit to New York, and *12th Floor* suggests more than mere anonymity. It could be any nondescript hotel in the city, though near enough to the Empire State Building and the then PanAm headquarters. The *12th Floor* part of the title (the Empire State Building has 102 storeys) does suggest he has clear perspective of the streets below.

Themes

There are several themes: isolation, helplessness, the lack of civilisation, urban violence and degradation, brutality, poverty and lack of progress from more primitive eras. It is also an attack on the nature of power and wealth.

Structure

First-person narration is used in all three verses, with each portraying different observations of, and reflections on, his visit to the largest city in the USA. There is an interesting use of **tense**: the first five lines are in the past tense, but line 6 begins the use of the present tense, making clear that it is now midnight.

Annotations

A Lines 1–4: 'I watched' makes clear the speaker's observer status; he is a spectator. The **simile** 'like a damaged insect' suggests the sheer size and scale of the Empire State Building – helicopters are not tiny, but beside the (then) tallest building in the world they look insect-like. That the insect is 'damaged' (line 2) suggests nature's difficulties in surviving in unnatural cities, while further suggesting that the symbol of innovative modern transport is so fragile that it is easily broken. The **metaphor** 'jumbo size dentist's drill' (line 4), highlighted by the **alliterative** 'd' sound, compares the Empire State Building, one of the most famous buildings and tourist attractions in the world, to a large 'dentist's drill', suggesting it looks huge, ugly and unpleasant. The image **connotes** pain – it is painful to be in New York, even by day.

Annotations (continued)

B Lines 6–9: in line 6, 'But' signals a change in time, especially by the use of the present tense. It is now 'Midnight', the upper-case 'M' suggesting **personification** – it has a mind of its own. That it 'has come in' suggests that midnight is invasive, uninvited, unwelcome, while 'from foreign places' suggests it is from somewhere unknown and dangerous, clearly linked to 'uncivilised darkness' (line 7), where 'uncivilised' connotes unacceptable, primitive, brutal behaviour and 'darkness' connotes something threatening, to be feared, where evil lurks. Although the word 'shot' indicates violence, it is 'a million lit windows' (line 8) shooting at the darkness to destroy it. The **contrast** of light and dark is reinforced by the personification and the alliteration of the 'l' sound ('million lit') as well as the assonance of the short 'i' sound in all three words. The theme of light (good) versus darkness (evil) is firmly established. The final line concludes the verse – the lit or unlit windows of the skyscrapers look like the 'ups and acrosses' (line 9) of a crossword puzzle, with no clues to help solve it. This puzzle is mysterious and unfathomable.

C Lines 10–11: in line 10, the 'But' at the beginning of the second verse signals the speaker's developing idea that midnight isn't easily conquered. The word 'not' is highlighted by being placed at the end of the line, creating the **enjambement** that emphasises the first three words of the next line.

D Lines 11–14: note also that the full stop and the comma in line 11 create two **caesurae** (breaks), which force the sentence to 'spill over' into the following line, emphasising that he is lying in bed between 'a radio and a television set' to drown out the noises from the city below; the 'wildest of warwhoops' (line 13) is a reference to the fearful war cries of the Native Americans during the battles with soldiers centuries before, as settlers moved the frontier west. In 'glittering canyons and gulches' (line 14), the alliteration of the **guttural**, hard 'g' and 'c' sounds, along with **assonance** of the short 'u' sounds, combine to establish a comparison of the violence of the Wild West and of the alleyways of modern New York. These are both metaphorical images comparing frontier battles to the noises of the city below. The expressions 'warwhoops' and 'ululating' are **onomatopoeic**, capturing the noises made by the Native Americans as well as the fearsome noises of New York.

E Lines 14–16: the dash at the end of line 14 helps focus on the noise from 'police cars and ambulances' as they rush to 'broken bones'. This is a **synecdochic** image of the injured on the streets – they are not regarded as people, just dehumanised 'bones'.

F Lines 15–18: the sounds of the modern city – the police cars and ambulances 'racing' – are much more urgent and distressing. In 'racing / to broken bones, the harsh screaming / from coldwater flats, the blood / glazed on the sidewalks' the **list** structure highlights the amount and range of cruelty and violence that is part of city life. The caesura after 'flats' (line 17) creates a break in the line structure, creating the enjambement that dramatically separates 'blood' from 'glazed on the sidewalks', forcing it onto a line by itself. This highlights and reinforces the **climax** to the verse. The use of historical and contemporary references in this verse develops not only the theme of evil and the lack of civilised behaviour in this modern, affluent city but also suggests that it has always been there – violence and evil are part of human nature.

G Lines 19–21: the last verse concludes the theme of violence developed throughout the poem. The idea that 'The frontier is never / somewhere else' (an extension of the Wild West metaphor) not only sums up the battle between the city of New York and the night, but also shows that within all humans there is the capacity for evil and violence – it's part of human nature. The use of 'And' (line 20) at the beginning of the final sentence effectively isolates, highlights and concludes the poem, making clear that no defence ('stockades') can prevent the advance of darkness, the symbol of unrelenting evil in human nature.

Question
Look at lines 6–9.
By referring to at least two examples of language, explain/analyse how the presence of evil is established.　　　　　2

The hospital smell
combs my nostrils
as they go bobbing along
green and yellow corridors.

A

5   What seems a corpse
is trundled into a lift and vanishes
heavenward.

B

I will not feel, I will not
feel, until

C

10   I have to.

D

Nurses walk lightly, swiftly,
here and up and down and there,

E

their slender waists miraculously
carrying their burden
15   of so much pain, so
many deaths, their eyes

F

still clear after
so many farewells.

Ward 7. She lies
20   in a white cave of forgetfulness.

G

A withered hand
trembles on its stalk. Eyes move

H

behind eyelids too heavy
to raise. Into an arm wasted
25   of colour a glass fang is fixed,

I

not guzzling but giving.
And between her and me
distance shrinks till there is none left

J

but the distance of pain that neither she nor I
30   can cross.

She smiles a little at this
black figure in her white cave

K

who clumsily rises
in the round swimming waves of a bell
35   and dizzily goes off, growing fainter,

L

not smaller, leaving behind only
books that will not be read
and fruitless fruits.

M

Context

As the speaker visits a loved one (or close friend) in hospital, he experiences apprehension and confusion as he walks to the ward. The person he is visiting is very ill and also seems to be similarly distressed.

Themes

The poem, though, like so much of MacCaig's poetry, resonates with the feelings of loss, sadness and pain that most of us experience when we visit a very ill relative or friend in hospital. The ending suggests that he is about to experience loss as well.

Structure

In *Visiting Hour*, the speaker reveals his feelings as he moves through the hospital to his friend's ward. The poem uses present tense, which creates immediacy, giving the reader access to the speaker's thoughts and feelings of sorrow and confusion.

Annotations

A Lines 1–4: the speaker begins with the recognisably strong, unique hospital smell. The **personification** 'combs my nostrils' suggests the smell is active and almost tactile. The image is **synecdochic**, as the word 'nostrils' is representing himself here. He develops the image by stating that 'they go bobbing along', as though his nostrils are dissociated from himself, again emphasising smell, though the word 'bobbing' is almost whimsical. The adjectives 'green and yellow' are **symbolic**, not only of illness, but also of his own upset emotions.

B Lines 5–7: while the phrase 'seems a corpse' suggests uncertainty, the word 'corpse' reminds us – and the speaker – of death. Yet 'trundled' conveys a lack of respect, while 'vanishes' suggests the absolute finality of death, though 'heavenward' is again mildly humorous, as MacCaig believed there was no life after death. The **enjambement** means 'heavenward' is in a line of its own, thereby drawing attention to the slightly mocking **tone**.

Annotations (continued)

C Lines 8–9: again, the use of enjambement causes the repetition of the word 'feel' to be in a new line, emphasising that he doesn't want to face his emotions. He is whispering to himself here, for reassurance.

D Lines 9–10: similarly, the use of enjambement splits 'until' from 'I have to', thereby drawing even more attention to denying his emotions at this stage.

E Lines 11–14: the two **adverbs** – 'lightly, swiftly' – suggest the nurses' casual, almost carefree, (perhaps also delicate) appearance. The **asyndetic** structure (no conjunctions) and the positioning of both **adjectives** at the end of the line suggests a speedy pace, heightened by the unusual word order of 'here and up and down and there' (the normal word order would be 'here and there, up and down') along with the use of **polysyndeton** (use of conjunctions). The word 'miraculously' suggests his amazement and wonder at their ability to carry such burdens, thereby further contributing to his feelings of confusion and inadequacy that such 'slender' nurses can be so strong – in **contrast** to the speaker, whose emotional burden by implication is great.

F Lines 15–18: he expands on what he sees as the nurses' burden: the **repetition** (anaphora) of the 'so much' as well as 'so many' draws attention to all that they deal with. Their clear eyes contrast his confusion and anxiety.

G Lines 19–20: the **minor sentence** 'Ward 7.' abruptly announces the speaker's arrival at his destination where his friend (referred to as 'she') lies 'in a white cave of forgetfulness', a **metaphor** where 'white' suggests the sheets and surroundings of the bed and 'cave' conveys her isolation from everyday existence. She is so ill she forgets everything.

H Lines 21–24: the metaphor 'withered' conveys the idea of something living that is now dying, dried out and shrivelled up. This is extended by the word 'stalk', which suggests that her wrist is frail and too weak to support her hand.

I Lines 25–26: note the **alliteration** in the vampiric image: the repetition of the **guttural** 'g' sound, along with the **fricative** 'f' sound, both create an unpleasant, harsh sound that captures the speaker's feeling of being upset by what he sees.

J Lines 27–30: this is a complex image, suggesting that though physically he is near her, emotionally he is far away from her. Neither of them can cross the barrier of pain between them.

K Lines 31–33: **contrast** is used effectively here: his 'black' appearance contrasts with her 'white' appearance, with 'white' signifying her illness and nearness to death, in contrast 'black' is signifying that he is alive. However, 'black' also has **connotations** of despondency, tying to the way he feels when he sees her so ill. His awkwardness is captured by the word 'clumsily'.

L Lines 34–36: **synaesthesia** (vision as sound) is used here, with the visual image of 'round swimming waves' as a feature of the sound made by the bell. This further increases his confusion, while 'swimming waves' almost suggests panic on his part at leaving her; 'fainter, / not smaller' could refer to the speaker or to the ill person, because as he moves away, he is getting fainter from her perspective but not smaller from his own.

M Lines 37–38: the books 'that will not be read' show that he realises that because she is dying she won't be able to read the books. The **oxymoron** 'fruitless fruits' is highlighted by the alliteration of the fricative ('f' sound) and by being in the concluding line. Fruit is a typical gift given to hospital patients, but because she won't survive to eat them, they will rot and decay. This is symbolic of her death to come, with the image further suggesting that his visit has been 'fruitless'.

Question

Look at lines 31–38.

By referring to at least two examples, explain/analyse how MacCaig uses contrast to convey the speaker's worry and upset.

4

Common Themes

Knowledge about themes is essential when it comes to dealing with the final 8-mark or 10-mark question at both N5 and Higher. MacCaig's poems cover a multiplicity of themes and each poem covers more than one theme, as shown by the table below.

Poem	Theme		
	Loss	Use of people and/or place to convey theme	Suffering
Assisi	Loss of compassion	Dwarf/Church of St Francis/priest	Poverty/lack of understanding/ sympathy
Aunt Julia	Speaker's loss of his aunt/loss of way of life	Aunt Julia and Luskentyre	Harshness of nature/ harshness of way of life
Basking Shark	Loss of closeness with nature	Basking shark and the sea	Ugliness of detachment from nature
Brooklyn Cop	Loss of civilised behaviour	Cop and Brooklyn	Ugliness of New York City streets/violence
Hotel Room, 12th Floor	Loss of humanity	New York in the 1960s	Ugliness of New York City life/violence
Visiting Hour	Loss of loved one/ death	Dying of his loved one and hospital	Ugliness of dying/ watching death

Isolation	Nature	Universal commentary on human existence or challenge to received ideas
The dwarf is isolated from the church	The references to birds and the varying relationships of people to them	Thoughtlessness of humans
The isolation of Aunt Julia's lifestyle and the isolation of Scotland's previous culture	The natural landscape	The disappearance of a previous way of life – the dislocation of modern Scotland from nature
The isolation of the speaker enabling his change in thinking	The difference between animal and human nature	The false superiority of humans
The isolation of the cop from civilised society	Human nature and violence	Good and evil – the suggestion that evil wins
The isolation of the speaker from the streets of New York	The difficulty of nature in an urban environment	The thought that violence is always there and can't be kept at bay
The isolation of the speaker within the hospital and the isolation of his friend within her illness	The relationship between life and death	Life is terminal and death inevitable

Isolation 1

You must be able to: discuss and analyse the theme of isolation in the poetry of Norman MacCaig.

Isolation is a major theme in all of MacCaig's poetry. Invariably, the speaker feels isolated, but even in *Basking Shark*, there is a sense in which the speaker feels that human beings have isolated themselves from nature.

Assisi

The poem is structured in three verses and uses **first-person narration**. The first verse is about the dwarf and his appalling disability, the second is about the priest and his lack of compassion, and the final verse is about the stupidity of the tourists, with a return to the dwarf at the end.

In *Assisi*, the speaker is the observer of all that happens 'outside the three tiers of churches built / in honour of St Francis', including the dwarf begging and the Church ignoring him. The recognised theme of this poem is the hypocrisy of the Church, which is seen in the priest, who, while showing the tourists **Giotto's** visual graphics of the teachings of the Bible and the Church, does nothing to help the suffering of the begging dwarf outside. But there is a darker message: the affluent Church is ignoring the poverty at its doors.

The poem is subtle. St Francis is a lover of birds, revealing the goodness in human nature. Meanwhile the tourists behave like birds, unthinkingly following the priest, revealing their stupidity. The three tiers of churches represent the honour in which goodness is held, with the 'ruined temple' representing the poverty, cruelty and neglect that some humans have to suffer.

Each verse ends with a surprising idea, one that makes the reader think. In the first verse, the dwarf is presented as an almost non-living, lifeless object – 'half-filled sack', 'twisted legs' and 'sawdust' all suggest that he is deformed and unhuman, weak and disintegrating. The speaker then uses contrast: the disabled, unfortunate dwarf is set beside the hugely magnificent 'three tiers of churches'. This contrast highlights the **irony** that the church was built to celebrate the very person who gave succour to the poor, yet the person who needs help – the dwarf – is ignored.

There is a bitterness in tone created by the **enjambement** – 'the advantage / of not being dead yet' – because, given the suffering of the dwarf, it is difficult to see how his being alive is an advantage. The final word of the verse is 'yet', suggesting that it won't be long until he is dead. This verse enhances the themes of suffering, poverty and death.

The second verse increases the underlying darkness in the poem in its presentation of the priest. He is made out to be superior, someone who places knowledge about art above alleviating the suffering of the poor. Irony is developed in the final sentence, with the final word 'cleverness' being used in a **pejorative** way – the speaker doesn't regard the priest as clever at all. Moreover, 'cleverness' can have the **connotation** of being artful.

The final verse presents the tourists using the **collective noun** – 'a rush of tourists' – suggesting that they behave as one body. The metaphor 'clucking contentedly' compares them to hens, birds renowned for their stupidity, suggesting that the tourists are mindless admirers. There is a further irony in the use of the food metaphor – 'grain of the Word': the priest 'feeds' the tourists, but no-one feeds the dwarf.

Throughout, the dwarf is presented as isolated from the activity and affluence surrounding him.

The **metaphor** 'ruined temple' suggests that the dwarf, like a temple, should be respected and treated with dignity, but he is crippled and ignored. The metaphor also works at another level, suggesting that the Church (as an institution) is a 'ruined temple', in that its original teachings and help that it gave the poor have become decayed over time and are now in ruins.

Yet, there is something disturbing and dark about the ending. To whom does he say 'Grazie' (all along he has been ignored)? Is it to the speaker? And is the dwarf's response – the **simile** comparing his reply to that of a child – proportionate to the donation? Is MacCaig being sarcastic? After all, the comparisons with the child and the mother, the bird and St Francis, both of which **connote** innocence and trust, seem as inappropriate as they are excessive.

Assisi is an attack on the hypocrisy of the Church and it is also an attack on poverty and neglect. The poem highlights the dwarf's poverty and neglect, but it also attacks the metaphorical poverty of the Church's forgotten purpose and lack of principles in the mid-20th century. The Church has become distracted from the lonely, ugly, destitute dwarf outside. The dwarf is a **synecdochic** representation of the neglected poor and the priest a synecdochic representation of the arrogance of the Church.

Question

With reference to *Assisi*, show how MacCaig conveys the theme of isolation.

Isolation 2

You must be able to: discuss and analyse the theme of isolation in the poetry of Norman MacCaig.

In *Assisi*, it is the dwarf and all that he symbolically represents who is isolated, but the theme is there in all MacCaig's poems. Isolation is not only geographical, it can be emotional and even universal: his poems suggest that it's part of the human condition to feel isolated. Sometimes this comes through loss, sometimes through suffering and even because human beings have an innate dark side to them.

Aunt Julia

In *Aunt Julia*, the speaker at the beginning is a young boy, obviously from the Lowlands, visiting his aunt on Harris in the West Highlands. By the last verse, the speaker is an adult, reflecting on the experience of visits to his aunt. The poem deals with isolation, loss and death, not only the loss and death of his aunt, but of the previous way of life in the isolated Highlands and Islands.

The isolated nature of the location (and of Aunt Julia) is immediately portrayed by the reference to Gaelic, the language his aunt spoke but he couldn't understand.

Isolation is also depicted by the 'absolute darkness / of a box bed' – she is so isolated that there are no lights nearby and the night-time is pitch black. The fact that the cottage is so small that the only spare bed is a box bed in the living room means that the place is devoid of luxuries.

The poverty of her existence is conveyed by the hardship she suffers. 'She was buckets' means that there was no running water and she had to collect water in buckets. '[Winds] pouring wetly' suggests the harshness of the weather and the lack of protection against the elements. The phrase 'keeper of threepenny bits' suggests her **frugality**, her need to save, all a measure of the poverty of her existence.

The most significant isolation is, of course, when Aunt Julia is 'in the absolute black / of a sandy grave'. But the poem is also a **synecdoche**, where Aunt Julia represents the death of a previous Scottish way of life which has passed with her. The speaker represents modern Scotland in this contrast. Their inability to communicate – 'so many questions / unanswered' – suggests that we will never really understand what has gone forever. The final word of the poem is isolated in a line by itself – the word 'unanswered'.

The poem, as with all of his poems, has universal significance. 'I hear her still' suggests more than just that he hears his Aunt Julia's voice in his imagination – it also suggests that we can all hear echoes of the voice of traditional Scotland, though we are no longer part of it. The speaker reinforces the point by his use of the present **tense**, and the 'hundred yards' across which he hears her voice represents the incredible distance between modern, urban Scotland and a way of life that we no longer know. There is, at the end of the poem, a tone of frustration shown by the repetition of 'angry', culminating in a tone of regret. The final last line perhaps indicates the speaker's regret about the passing of that way of life, though he can do nothing about it.

Visiting Hour

Visiting Hour is also about isolation and loss. The speaker feels isolated, dissociated even, confused and nervous as he visits a dying friend in the hospital. Like *Aunt Julia and Assisi*, death isn't far away, and for the speaker nothing is more isolating than death.

His feelings of confusion are highlighted in the fourth verse, where he feels isolated in himself from what he sees as capable nurses, who walk 'lightly, swiftly', unencumbered by the pain that surrounds them. The **polysyndeton** – 'here and up and down and there' – along with the abnormal arrangement of the phrases, emphasises the nurses' speed and the ability to always be where they are needed, unlike the speaker, who is aware of 'so much pain, so / many deaths, their eyes / still clear'. The **anaphora** in the repetition of 'so much' draws our attention, further intensified by the repetition of the **intensifier** 'so' to the pain he feels so keenly in comparison to the nurses.

The isolation is emphasised in the fifth verse: he states that 'she lies in a white cave of forgetfulness' suggesting that, because of her illness, she cannot remember who he is, and is utterly isolated.

But perhaps the greatest isolation that is expressed is when he 'goes off, growing fainter, / not smaller'. This is a complex image that suggests from the patient's perspective he seems faint, out of focus, but from his own perspective he isn't any smaller in stature. He feels isolated by her imminent death.

> ### Question
>
> With reference to *Aunt Julia* and *Visiting Hour*, show how MacCaig conveys the theme of isolation.

You must be able to: discuss and analyse the theme of nature in the poetry of Norman MacCaig.

Nature is another important theme in MacCaig's poetry. He observes and explores not only nature itself (as in *Aunt Julia*), but also human nature.

Basking Shark

Of all six poems, *Basking Shark* explores and reflects most on nature, both human and animal. The speaker is in a rowing boat out at sea when he unexpectedly encounters a basking shark.

The use of rhyming triplets throughout the poem gives the poem a very tight feel, in keeping with the intensity of the speaker's thinking throughout. The **rhymes** throughout are pure rhymes, echoing the closeness of the thought process.

He begins by referring to the shark as a monster – 'with a matchbox brain': the speaker feels superior. But he soon states that the shark 'displaced more than water', a **metaphor** suggesting that the displacement was in his thinking. The central **image** of the poem occurs in the third verse, when he states 'this decadent townee / Shook on a wrong branch of his family tree'. This is a self-mocking image, where he sees the dislocation between mankind's hedonistic urban existence and the natural world as the problem. We are 'Shook on the wrong branch' of the family tree: we are an evolutionary aberration or deviation. The word 'shook' further suggests that our mistaken position on 'the wrong branch' is precarious, uncertain.

He concludes by asking the rhetorical question: 'who's the monster?'. The implied answer is that we are – human beings are monstrous. Our nature has developed in the wrong direction because we have lost touch with the 'slime of everything', with the origins of life, with nature itself and therefore have no reason to feel that we are the superior species.

Hotel Room, 12th Floor

In *Hotel Room, 12th Floor*, MacCaig again explores the dislocation between nature and human beings, though in this poem he goes on to suggest that, although we have built a powerful 'civilisation', we are no more civilised now than we were in the days of the 'wildest of warwhoops continually ululating through / the glittering canyons and gulches'. The comparison between the Wild West and the streets of New York, with 'blood / glazed on the sidewalks', makes clear that the violence and 'uncivilised darkness' have more to do with human nature than the urbanisation of America: the place has always been violent because violence is rooted in human nature, and isn't caused by the environment.

The very opening of the poem reveals the effect of the city on nature, with the 'helicopter skirting like a damaged insect'. The simile compares the helicopter, a **synecdochic** representation of technology, to a 'damaged insect', a representation of the difficulty that nature has surviving in unnatural cities.

But, like *Assisi*, this poem also deals with poverty by portraying the gap between those symbols of power and wealth – the Empire State Building (the tallest building in the world at the time) and the PanAm skyscraper (the most powerful airline at the time) – and the poor, destined to live in 'coldwater flats', which represented the most destitute of living conditions for New York's underprivileged.

Brooklyn Cop

This poem is different in that there is no speaker as such, no first person, but there is an observer who comments on what he sees on the streets of Brooklyn. *Brooklyn Cop* observes and examines human nature very closely and directly. In it MacCaig portrays human beings as violent as they are fearful. The cop may be 'Built like a gorilla', with all the **connotations** of aggression and strength, but in the morning, when leaving his wife, 'he said, "See you, babe"', making clear that 'he hoped it, he truly hoped it'. The possibility that he might not return is clearly real.

But it's the end of the poem, when the observer refers to the cop 'whose home is a place / he might, this time, never get back to', that is a comment on human nature: the streets of a city are so perilous that even the police are unsafe. But it is also by referring to the cop's 'victims' that the line between good and evil is blurred.

> ## Question
>
> With reference to *Basking Shark* or *Hotel Room, 12th Floor*, show how MacCaig uses nature as a feature of his poetry.

You must be able to: discuss and analyse the theme of the dark side of human beings in the poetry of Norman MacCaig.

As always with MacCaig's poems there is an underlying dark side, often in the form of violence, of the uncivilised side to human beings. It is there in *Assisi*, *Basking Shark*, *Hotel Room, 12th Floor*, and is the dominant theme in *Brooklyn Cop*.

Brooklyn Cop

There are many references to violence, the hallmark of uncivilised behaviour. The speaker talks of the 'two / hieroglyphs in his face', scars that are symbols representing the violence he has suffered, though the 'trouble' that they mean is ambiguous: trouble for him (obviously) but trouble for others too, as he was the one who survived the attack. There is also a reference to the 'tissue over violence'. He is compared to a 'gorilla', with its reputation for strength and violence. He could 'plunge through / into violence' – suggesting that the descent into violence isn't far away. The repetition of 'gorilla', though this time with the addition of 'with a nightstick', intensifies the violence. The enigmatic ending: 'And who would be who have to be / his victims', where the criminals are referred to as 'his victims', suggests that there is not much difference between good and evil, signifying the darkness that lurks beneath the surface in us all.

Hotel Room, 12th Floor

In *Hotel Room, 12th Floor*, the speaker observes from his hotel room the dark evil of city life, which is a measure of the darkness that is part of our nature. The **simile** of the helicopter appearing 'like a damaged insect' suggests that urban life (symbolised by 'the Empire State Building') is hostile towards nature – we have created an environment that is almost anti-nature. Human beings have lost sight of what life, in all its senses, is about; urban settings are dark places, false and the opposite of natural environments.

But the speaker's point about the dark side of human beings is made all the more incisive when he personifies 'Midnight', with its associations of darkness and evil, especially coming in from 'foreign places', where in this context 'foreign' has connotations of the unknown, the strange and fearful, and also in his use of 'uncivilised darkness', where the word 'darkness' connotes evil, and the adjective 'uncivilised' reinforces the idea of cruel, intolerable behaviour.

The theme of darkness is summed up in the final verse of the poem where MacCaig suggests that the 'frontier' – the border between good and evil, dating back to the Wild West and the battles between early settlers and native Americans – underlies and is a consequence of humanity's evil intolerance. In 'no stockades / can keep the midnight out' we find a despairing comment that there is no protective barrier to keep evil at bay.

Assisi

In this poem, again MacCaig makes clear the intolerance of human beings, who allow poverty, discrimination and suffering to co-exist with wealth and extravagance. The dwarf represents not only a crippled, miserable, ugly person but is a symbol of privation (hardship) and destitution. On the other hand, the priest and the tourists represent not just a comfortable existence but such self-obsession and self-centredness that the plight of others is ignored by them. They don't even notice the dwarf. Although the priest and the tourists are not in themselves evil, they do represent the darkness of human beings because they display a lack of humanity as well as a lack of humility and an inability to recognise the desperate plight of others, aspects of human behaviour that are even more relevant in the 21st century.

Basking Shark

It is the word 'monster' that so interestingly shifts its meaning in this poem. To begin with, the speaker refers to the shark as that 'roomsized monster with a matchbox brain', indicating that he sees the shark as primeval (ancient and prehistoric) with a tiny brain. There is a tone of superiority in his language, especially shown in his use of alliteration. But as he recognises that this 'decadent townee', the representative of human beings, is 'Shook on a wrong branch of his family tree', he realises that maybe we have made a mistake, and our position on the 'family tree' (the tree of life) is precarious, uncertain. The darkness in this poem isn't so much the evil in our nature, but the idea that we have lost sight of what it is to be part of nature – we have become lost – and as he asks himself 'So who's the monster?' he already knows the answer. Although, this time 'monster' takes on different **connotations**, suggesting something ugly and frighteningly destructive.

> ### Question
>
> With reference to *Brooklyn Cop*, show how MacCaig examines the dark side of human nature.

Common Techniques

Poem	Sound Effects	Enjambement/ Sentence Structure	Imagery		
			Comparison/ Central Image	Representation/ Symbolism	Contrast
Assisi	✓	p44, p51	✓	p48	p49
Aunt Julia	✓	p50	✓	p48	p49
Basking Shark	p43	p45, p51	p46	✓	✓
Brooklyn Cop	p43	✓	✓	p48	✓
Hotel Room, 12th Floor	✓	p50	✓	p48	✓
Visiting Hour	p43	p44, p50	p47	p48	p49

Poetic techniques used in MacCaig's poetry

The table opposite outlines the use of common techniques in all six poems, with page references to specific examples in this book (a tick (✓) indicates that a technique is used in a poem but is not discussed in detail).

The term **free verse** refers to poems that do not have regular **rhythm** or **rhyme**. In a sense, the verse isn't 'free' since MacCaig pays so much attention to **enjambement** or **line breaks**: he structures lines not only to capture the rhythms of everyday speech but also to highlight the points he makes and therefore the theme. He uses rhythm to capture the pauses and pulses of spoken English. Enjambement is where the important unit of sense is the sentence and not necessarily the line structure. In all his poems, pay attention to MacCaig's use of enjambement and line breaks. *Basking Shark* is the only one of the six poems to have a **rhyme scheme**.

Themes are conveyed by techniques. In the Scottish Text section of the Critical Reading paper, most of the questions will be about language, a term which covers sentence structure, **contrast, imagery, word choice** and **tone**. Some questions ask about a specific technique, such as word choice or imagery. You need also to be aware of techniques that are associated with poetry, such as particular sound effects and enjambement, which you may want to refer to in your answers.

You need to be able to analyse the effectiveness of various images: for example, **metaphor, simile** or **personification**. But these aren't the only images – there is also **synecdoche, symbolism, oxymoron** and **onomatopoeia**.

These different techniques can be classified: there are three major poetic techniques (although they aren't restricted to poetry):

- devices of comparison

- devices of representation

- devices of contrast (or **paradox**).

You also need to know about rhythm, which is an important technique in poetry.

Sound Effects

You must be able to: discuss and analyse the use of sound effects in the poetry of Norman MacCaig.

Vowel sounds and consonant sounds

Sound is an important aspect of both poetry and prose. By the word 'sound', we mean the sound that we make when we speak.

There are five main vowels in English – *a, e, i, o* and *u*. We can pronounce those vowels as in *hate, feed, pine, slope* and *cute*. These are known as long vowel sounds. We can also pronounce these same vowels with a short vowel sound as in *hat, fed, pin, slop* and *cut*. Long vowel sounds tend to be more pleasant than short vowel sounds.

The other letters of the alphabet are known as consonants. Consonants can be grouped, according to the type of sound they make, as shown in the table below.

Letter	Example	Type of sound	Effect of sound
b and p	bang	plosive	hard, violent
hard c, hard g, qu and k	cat, goal, queen, kill	guttural	harsh, unpleasant, violent
d and t	dentist, tooth	dental	neutral, depends on vowel sound
f, th and v	face, that, verse	fricative	can be unpleasant, depends on vowel sound
l, w and y	liquid, wool, you	liquid	mellifluous and pleasant, but the *w* sound can be mean
m and n	the murmur of innumerable (bees)	nasal	usually pleasant, but can be unpleasant when adenoidal
soft c, s and z	cell, silence, zodiac, snake, hiss	sibilant	soporific or hissing
r	reef	rolling	almost like a vowel
soft g and j	slounge, television (even softer than 'age', much softer then 'jam')	a more vocalised, softer sibilant	usually a pleasant sound

The repetition of a vowel sound is called **assonance** (for example, the short 'u' sound in 'clubbings' and 'gunshots') while the repetition of a consonant is called **alliteration** (for example, 'clucking contentedly').

Onomatopoeia is where the sound of a word imitates the sound to which it refers – for example, 'bang' represents a sudden explosive noise. MacCaig frequently uses onomatopoeia, as well as the other sound devices of alliteration and assonance.

Onomatopoeia is used in *Basking Shark* with the second word of the poem – 'stub'. The use of the short 'u' sound and the violent **plosive** (the 'b' sound) creates a violent word that replicates the noise of his oar hitting what the speaker thought was a rock. There is also 'slounge', another onomatopoeic word, capturing the sound of the large shark easing upwards out of the water, with the long vowel 'ou' combining with the soft 'g' sound to support the meaning.

In *Brooklyn Cop*, 'clubbings' and the 'Wham' of 'Whamburger' are onomatopoeic as is 'warwhoops' and 'ululating' in *Hotel Room, 12th Floor*, all of which replicate the sound of violence.

MacCaig also uses alliteration and assonance, both powerful sound devices. The following example of alliteration is from *Visiting Hour*:

> a **g**lass **f**ang is **f**ixed,
> not **g**uzzling but **g**iving

Although the 'g's in 'fang', 'guzzling' and 'giving' are not pronounced (not in Scotland anyway), nevertheless they form an almost visual alliteration, which is still effective in drawing attention to the image – the guttural 'g' is also a harsh sound, which, along with the fricative, add to the shock of the image, revealing the shock felt by the speaker when he saw the intravenous drip.

The pure rhymes of *Basking Shark* are achieved by the use of assonance. Assonance is also used in the last line of *Visiting Hour*:

> and **fru**itless **fru**its

The assonance along with the oxymoron together highlight the fruitlessness – pointlessness – of the speaker's visit and the anguish he feels at her probable death.

Question

With reference to *Assisi*, show how MacCaig's use of alliteration at the beginning of the poem helps draw attention to the dwarf's deformities.

Enjambement

You must be able to: discuss and analyse the use of enjambement in the poetry of Norman MacCaig.

Always pay attention to where **line breaks** take place.

Traditionally, a line of poetry is **end-stopped**: the line is complete in itself, thus creating a 'pause' for the reader at the end of each line.

In some poems, however, poets use a technique known as **enjambement** or run-on or spill-over lines, where one line spills over onto the next. For example, look at the first verse from *Assisi*, where the first line 'spills over' onto the next:

> The dwarf with his hands on backwards
> sat,

MacCaig breaks the line after 'backwards' thereby isolating and drawing attention to the word 'sat'. Indeed, all the lines spill from one to the next. Enjambement is a structural technique where the continuation of a sentence goes beyond the line's end. A break in a syntactical unit (such as a sentence) causes a phrase, clause or sentence to run on from one line to the next or from one verse to the next.

Often, the poet uses a **caesura** or pause somewhere near the middle of the line in order to force the sentence to 'spill over' or break. Look at this example from *Visiting Hour*:

> I will not feel, I will not
> feel, until
> I have to.

Note the caesura – the pause – in the first and second line: in each case, the mid-line pause forces the sentence to spill over from line 1 to line 2 and then onto line 3. Try reading this verse in lines and you'll see that it doesn't make sense. You must read it as a sentence, paying little attention to the line structure, to make sense of what MacCaig is saying. Though you pay little attention to line structure, you still pay some attention. Because this is poetry, you cannot help, however briefly, to hesitate at the end of the line (the line break) and that causes the beginning of the next line to come as a surprise, or shock, even. In this case, the word 'feel' is emphasised by being forced onto the beginning of the second line, thereby drawing attention to the speaker's determination to keep his emotions under control.

Effects of enjambement

- Because we are used to pausing at the end of a line, we hesitate a bit, which makes what comes at the beginning of the next line a surprise – sometimes we are taken aback.

- Often enjambement reflects the thoughts of the person as he or she recounts the experience being presented. For example, in *Visiting Hour*, the enjambement reflects and captures the speaker's thoughts as he moves through the hospital to visit his loved one. The reader is thereby given access to the man's feelings.

- Because enjambement prioritises sentence structure over line structure, the poem reads more like prose, making it more accessible to the reader.

MacCaig uses the technique of enjambement frequently. Combined with his use of enjambement, his use of **rhythm** and simple words make his poems highly accessible. But do not be deceived: although he makes poetry seem simple and straightforward, there is always a deeper meaning than first appears.

The following example is from *Basking Shark*:

> Swish up the dirt and, when it settles, a spring
> Is all the clearer. I saw me, in one fling,
> Emerging from the slime of everything.

The language here seems very straightforward: there are after all only four multisyllabic words, two of which are only dissyllabic (words of two syllables). But the enjambement means that attention is drawn to 'is all the clearer', which, by being separated from 'a spring' makes the reader realise that the expression is **metaphorical**. Not only is the sea clearer but so is his thinking. This makes the reader realise that 'swish up the dirt' isn't just a **kinetic image**, it is metaphorical, suggesting that the behaviour of the shark disturbed and confused his thinking, until everything becomes clearer.

The caesura in the second line forces the **parenthetical** 'in one fling' to the end of the line, thereby drawing attention to not only the speed with which he has the thought, but also his amusement at realising that all life emerged from 'slime', that we all come from the same thick, wet, sludge, millions of years ago, with the implication that human beings have the same origin as all other animals. The language may look uncomplicated, but the use of enjambement helps the complexity of this thinking emerge.

 Question

Look carefully at the last three lines of *Aunt Julia*.

Show how MacCaig uses enjambement effectively.

Imagery: Comparison

You must be able to: discuss and analyse the use of comparison.

Devices of comparison include **metaphor, simile** and **personification**. In these techniques, one thing is compared to another: 'The boy was like a tiger in the fight', where 'The boy' is being compared to a tiger in his ability to fight.

Often you are asked to demonstrate the effectiveness of a metaphor (or simile or personification). In order to do so, first of all think about the **literal** meaning of the term to which the comparison is made – in this case 'a tiger'. How does a tiger fight? Work out all the **connotations**, and, if the boy fought viciously, fiercely, ferociously then the metaphor is appropriate and therefore effective.

Read the following lines from *Basking Shark* by MacCaig:

> I count as gain
> That once I met, on a sea tin-tacked with rain,
> That roomsized monster with a matchbox brain.

There are three metaphors in these lines. He describes the sea 'tin-tacked with rain'. He talks of the 'roomsized monster' and its 'matchbox brain'. The first one doesn't appear at first glance as a comparison. He isn't comparing the sea with anything, but he is comparing the shape the rain makes as it drops onto the surface of the sea: the shape looks like the shape of a tin-tack.

Sometimes an **image** is so stunningly accurate that it becomes unforgettably implanted in your memory, like this one about the 'sea tin-tacked with rain'. A tin-tack is a drawing pin, and if you can imagine it upside down, with the flat bit of the drawing pin downwards, then you have the mental picture of each raindrop – the pin of the drawing pin – hitting the sea and thereby causing a tiny circular wave – the flat bit of the pin – on the surface of the sea.

When you want to analyse the effect of an image, it often helps to start with the literal meaning. Once you have established that, you can then use the relevant connotations suggested to you by the literal meaning to show the effectiveness of the metaphor.

The other metaphors – 'roomsized monster' and 'matchbox brain' – are also to do with shape. We associate rooms with being large (certainly larger than a basking shark), which means that this comparison is effective because it suggests the shape of the animal, but it is also effective because it is an exaggeration – a **hyperbole** – another kind of comparison. Hyperbole can also often be amusing, and there is something light-hearted about the exaggerated use of 'roomsized' and 'matchbox'.

Moreover, 'matchbox brain' suggests the minute size (a matchbox isn't big) of the animal's brain, signifying not only its diminutive capacity, but also its primordiality.

In *Visiting Hour*, the second verse uses metaphor:

> What seems a corpse
> is trundled into a lift and vanishes
> heavenward.

The metaphor is 'vanishes heavenward': the corpse doesn't actually vanish, and it isn't going to heaven, as MacCaig did not believe in an afterlife. But the metaphor is a kind of joke, where he is mocking those who believe that when we die we go somewhere else.

He uses metaphor at the beginning of the fifth verse:

> She lies
> in a white cave of forgetfulness

She isn't literally in a cave, but the term with its adjective 'white' suggests the idea of her surrounded by white sheets and curtains. However, the metaphor also creates the idea that the 'white cave' is her mind, which remembers very little.

 Question

Look at *Basking Shark*.

Show how MacCaig uses metaphor in the third and fourth verses of the poem.

Imagery: Representation and Contrast

You must be able to: discuss and analyse the use of representation and contrast in the poetry of Norman MacCaig.

Devices of representation

Synecdoche is a device of representation in which a part of something represents the whole or something larger. An example of synecdoche is a company's logo, where a small badge or even a word represents the entire company and its values. In a film, a vulture circling overhead can represent death.

For example, in line 7 of *Hotel Room, 12th Floor*, the term 'from foreign places' represents places of conflict that are unknown and threatening. MacCaig quite frequently uses synecdoche.

In *Visiting Hour*, the word 'corpse' is a synecdochic representation of death, revealing what the speaker associates with hospitals as well as his own fear of what he might find.

In *Assisi*, the 'three tiers of churches' is a representation of all that St Francis stood for and believed in – compassion, understanding and the desire to help. It can also be seen as an elaborate, expensive and inappropriate representation of St Francis' simple beliefs in goodness and kindness.

Aunt Julia has many examples of synecdoche – in lines 17–23, for example, there are several. The image 'She was buckets' is synecdochic: 'buckets' represents the harshness of her lifestyle, as she has to fetch water to her croft.

Symbolism is also a device of representation. But what is the difference between symbolism and synecdoche? Symbols are quite random. We know that red roses symbolise love, but what is it about a red rose that suggests love? Nothing. The image is random, but we accept it as a symbol because it is culturally established. Although symbolism is a device of representation, the relationship between the signifier (in this case, a rose) and the signified (in this case, love) is purely arbitrary.

In contrast, synecdoche isn't at all arbitrary: synecdoche is the use of a small part of an object or image to represent the larger entity. An example is 'All hands on deck', where 'hand' represents the entire sailor. In *Visiting Hour*, for example, 'nostrils' is a synecdochic image: they represent his entire body.

Be relaxed about your use of these terms: Aunt Julia, herself, the character presented in the poem, is symbolic of a way of life that has died. In *Assisi*, the 'three tiers of churches' is symbolic of the church as an institution, just as the cop in *Brooklyn Cop* symbolises the danger and violence of New York streets. Places and characters tend to be symbolic, whereas parts representing a bigger whole are synecdochic.

Devices of contrast

MacCaig often uses the device of **contrast** – indeed he uses it in all six poems.

In *Aunt Julia*, for example, there is contrast between the 'absolute darkness' of the box bed in lines 14–15, in which the speaker slept as a young boy, and the 'absolute black' (line 28) of his aunt's sandy grave. The darkness of the bed is comforting, whereas the grave is black, suggesting the depressing finality of death.

Contrast is also used in *Assisi*, especially between the 'ruined temple' and the grandiose 'three tiers of churches': the effect is to highlight the desperation of the dwarf against the symbol of religion. Contrast is also used to highlight the physical ugliness and disgusting appearance of the dwarf to St Francis in the first verse and to the child in the final verse. Contrast is also used to highlight the difference between the dwarf's outward appearance ('lopsided mouth') and his kindness, politeness and inner beauty.

Contrast is an important technique throughout *Visiting Hour*. There is the contrast between his feelings of insecurity and how he sees the nurses with their ability to cope with their feelings. The contrast exposes his shock when he sees what he describes as a 'glass fang', with its **connotations** of fatal bite and even the living dead, contrasting with the idea that it is this fang that keeps her alive. And, of course, the contrast between his 'black figure' in 'her white cave', suggesting his sombre appearance beside her ill figure.

Oxymoron is a form of contrast. Technically oxymoron is the **juxtaposition** (placing side-by-side) of terms that are apparently contradictory – but only apparently. For example, 'parting is such sweet sorrow', where 'sweet' and 'sorrow' would appear to contradict each other, but parting from someone close to you is sorrowful because you will miss him or her, but it can also be sweet because the future may bring better times.

MacCaig's most famous oxymoron is found in the last line of *Visiting Hour*: 'fruitless fruits'. These two words seem opposites, yet, if you look deeper into the image, you can see that the giving of fruit to his dying friend is 'fruitless', as she won't survive to eat them. From the speaker's perspective, however, the visit itself was fruitless as she scarcely recognised him or knew he was there.

> ## Question
>
> Look at *Hotel Room, 12th Floor*.
>
> Show how one example of contrast is used by MacCaig in this poem.

Rhythm and Sentence Structure

You must be able to: discuss and analyse the use of rhythm in the poetry of Norman MacCaig.

Although MacCaig tends not to use regular **rhythm**, nevertheless the use of rhythm that is closest to everyday speech is an important technique of his poetry. There is the rhythm of the individual line, but also the rhythm of entire sentences, which can spill over from line to line (**enjambement**). But, and this is important, although the lines 'spill over', nevertheless there is a **line break**, which is an important device because it highlights the word or phrase in the next line, emphasising it. Rhythm is the modulation (variation in sound) of our voices as we speak. To identify MacCaig's use of rhythm, try to work out where the stress comes in each word. For example, when we say the word 'coffee', we stress the first syllable – '**cof**fee'. MacCaig exploits rhythm to replicate speech so that what is said supports the aspect of human experience that he is exploring. An important effect is that his use of rhythm makes his poetry more like prose and therefore more accessible to the reader.

Another important aspect of arrangement in poetry is the use of verse structure. MacCaig does not use **rhyme** – with the exception of *Basking Shark* – and though he does not employ regular rhythm, he uses what are referred to as **verse paragraphs**, where one verse leads on from the previous while exploring a different aspect of content.

In *Visiting Hour*, the rhythm throughout is of a speaker relating his thoughts to himself in such a way that the reader has access to everything he is going through – his fears, his attempts not to feel, his strong sense of confusion when he sees how easily the nurses deal with pain and death. Much of the success of the poem is the rhythm created in part by the enjambement.

In *Aunt Julia*, the whole of the poem, but in particular verse 4 (lines 17–23), uses rhythm, mainly created by enjambement, to echo and replicate the rhythms of speech. One of the major effects is not just to give us access to what the speaker is thinking and feeling, but it also gives us access to what kind of person he is.

A major part of MacCaig's success is his ability to use the rhythms of speech to create poetry that resonates with all of us. More than that though, it is his ability to use language and its rhythms to expose an underlying darkness in human experience. For example, in *Hotel Room, 12th Floor*, the use of language and rhythm in the last verse exposes his idea that the battle between good and evil is everywhere and there is no defence against evil.

Look at the lines:

> The frontier is never
> somewhere else. And no stockades
> can keep the midnight out.

There are two **declarative sentences**: the first states that the borderline between good and evil is ever present, just as much today as in earlier eras – it is always with us. However, the second statement makes it clear that no 'stockades' – that is, defence barriers – can keep 'midnight' (evil) out because evil is part of human nature. Listen to the apparent simplicity of the rhythm: the repetition of the negatives 'never' and 'no' emphasises that it is a losing battle, and beginning the last sentence with 'And' draws attention to and isolates the finality of the point that evil cannot be defeated – it will always come in from 'foreign places'. The line break after 'stockades' forces 'can keep the midnight out' into the final line, thus creating the **climax** – evil is always present.

In *Basking Shark*, too, he uses rhythm and rhyme to create a more 'poetic' feel than in other of his poems. In the first two verses, most of the lines are **end-stopped**, an entirely poetic technique. Here he is less concerned about reflecting the rhythms of everyday speech, though by the third verse, the enjambement helps create rhythms closer to spoken English. Rhyme also makes the poem more 'poetic', reflecting the more philosophical subject matter.

It is by means of sentence structure and enjambement that MacCaig is able to capture the rhythm of everyday speech. For example, in *Assisi*, the opening verse if read aloud sounds as though it is prose. This is achieved by his use of rhythm created by the enjambement. The spill-over of the first few lines takes away the 'poetic' feel, making the poem very accessible.

Question

Look at *Brooklyn Cop*.

Show how MacCaig uses rhythm and sentence structure to suggest the violence that the speaker witnesses.

Quick tips

The Critical Reading paper consists of two sections.

Section (marks)	Assessment
Section 1 (20)	Questions assess understanding, analysis and evaluation of previously studied Scottish texts from the specified list, covering the genres of drama, prose and poetry. There will be poems and extracts from each writer.
Section 2 (20)	Critical essay questions assess understanding, analysis and evaluation of previously studied texts from drama, prose, poetry, film and television or language. **Candidates will select ONE question from a genre different from the one chosen in Section 1.**

If you are studying two Scottish texts – one text (drama or prose) or a set of poems for section 1 – then you **must** choose a **different genre** to write about in the critical essay in section 2.

If you choose to use Norman MacCaig for the Critical Essay section, then make sure that you read more widely than the six poems specified for the Scottish Text section: *Sparrow*, *Return to Scalpay*, *Ringed Plover by a Water's Edge* and *Two Focuses* are good examples, along with *Memorial* and *Sounds of the Day*.

In the Critical Reading exam, for section 1 you will be given a printed poem by Norman MacCaig and a set of questions totalling 20 marks.

For section 2 you will be given a series of general questions (on drama, prose, poetry, film and television drama, and language). You will choose one question and use your chosen text to write an essay that answers the question. Again, the question is worth 20 marks.

Make sure that you understand what the question is asking. Most questions in section 1 will ask about language; 'language' includes sentence structure, word choice, imagery, contrast and tone as well as structural techniques, such as verse structure, rhyme (where appropriate), rhythm, sentence structure, enjambement and contrast. 'Language' also includes the sounds of the words, that is, the use of alliteration, assonance and onomatopoeia.

You should spend about 45 minutes on each section.

When writing answers to questions in section 1, there is no need to write in paragraphs – it is better to use bullet points. Make your answers as precise and analytical as you can.

Do keep checking back to the question. N5 and Higher exams are tests of reading skills – make sure you read the question carefully and accurately.

If your answer is vague, the chances are you're missing the point. Be as concise as you can.

There are three important differences between N5 questions and Higher questions.

- In N5, there is credit for all quotations/references but not in Higher.

- N5 questions use the word 'explain', for example: 'By referring to two examples of language, explain how the writer ...'. However, in Higher, although the formula is similar, the word 'analyse' is often (but not always) used, for example: 'By referring to at least two examples, analyse how ...'. Sometimes the Higher question is framed like this: 'Analyse how the poet's language creates a change in mood'.

- In N5 the final question is worth 8 marks whereas at Higher the final question is worth 10 marks.

In the Higher question formula, it is worth heeding the advice to use at least two examples. Since there are no marks for quotation/reference, you have to give a 'detailed/insightful comment plus quotation/reference' in order to gain 2 marks. For a more basic comment plus quotation/reference you gain 1 mark. There are 0 marks for quotation/reference alone. Therefore, for a question worth 4 marks, it is probably wiser to give three or four examples, rather than only two.

Know the poems

Preparation for the Scottish Text section is of utmost importance. It isn't enough to look at other people's annotations of poems, you really need to have a blank copy of each poem and make your own notes – the act of writing helps commit points to memory.

Also, you need to be very familiar with each poem – record the poems on your smartphone or tablet and listen to them at every opportunity; the act of listening helps commit the poems to memory, which will make it easier and quicker to support your comments with relevant quotes, especially when you have to refer to unseen poems in the 8- and 10-mark questions.

The questions

In answering the shorter questions (that is, other than the 8- and 10-mark questions), you need to be able to refer to the relevant section of the poem and then give a relevant close analytical comment.

Read the questions carefully. Both N5 and Higher papers are tests of reading skills, therefore if you make a mistake in reading a question, you will lose marks. It is useful to underline the parts of the text that you are going to quote and analyse in your answers.

Questions will be worth either 2 marks or 4 marks.

N5
- For a 2-mark question you must make one textual reference and a comment.

- For a 4-mark question you must make two textual references, each with a comment.

H
- For a 2-mark question you must make a textual reference and more detailed comments since references score 0 marks.

- For a 4-mark question you could make four textual references with four comments OR two textual references each with two detailed comments.

8- and 10-mark questions

Exam questions are designed to test your understanding of the themes and techniques of MacCaig's poetry and to test if you can show understanding of more than one poem.

The question will refer you to the given poem and ask you to make reference to **at least** one other poem. For the 8- and 10-mark questions, follow this procedure:

- 2 marks are given for identifying the 'commonality' between the given poem and your chosen poem(s) as identified in the question. The question could be about theme, characterisation, a central relationship, setting, place, symbolism, imagery, personal experience, narrative technique, rhyme and/or rhythm or any other important element of poetry.

  o Identify the feature as expressed in the question (from the list above), then relate that feature to another poem or poems by the same poet.

  o You in effect are stating what you see in common between the given poem and the other poem(s) chosen by you. Mention the second poem (or the third or more).

  o If the question is about theme, it can be useful to refer to the universal aspect of the theme, as it relates to the human condition.

- 2 marks are given for reference to the given extract, commenting on whatever has been identified in the question (whether theme, characterisation, setting, symbolism, etc.). In other words, you must deal with theme and/or a technique as listed above.

  N5 o In N5, there is 1 mark for the reference and 1 mark for the comment.

  H o In Higher, there are no marks for the reference, only for the comment(s).

  Make sure that the references you make can be supported by your knowledge of similar points in your chosen poem(s). Make sure that you refer to the text to support every point that you make.

- Both the N5 and Higher ask very similar questions at this stage. The difference is in the allocation of marks: in N5 there are 4 marks for comparing the given poem to one of your choice, whereas in Higher there are 6 marks for comparing the given poem to one of your choice.

N5 - 4 marks are given for references to another poem.

  o There is 1 mark for reference and 1 mark for comment, which means you need to make two references and one basic comment for each reference.

H - 6 marks are given for references to another poem or poems, with all marks dependent on the quality of your comments.

  o There are 0 marks for reference and 1 mark for analytical comment, which means you need to make six references and six basic (but analytical) comments.

  o Or you can give three references with more insightful or developed analyses (which gain 2 marks each).

Sample 8-mark and 10-mark questions

By referring to *Brooklyn Cop* and at least one other poem, show/discuss how the poet uses imagery effectively to convey themes.

By referring to *Basking Shark* and at least one other poem, show/discuss how MacCaig explores the relationship between human beings and nature.

By referring to *Aunt Julia* and at least one other poem, show/discuss how MacCaig explores the theme of isolation.

By referring to *Hotel Room, 12th Floor* and at least one other poem, show/discuss how MacCaig uses place as a feature of his poetry.

By referring to *Visiting Hour* and at least one other poem, show/discuss how MacCaig uses contrast to portray themes in his poetry.

By referring to *Assisi* and at least one other poem, show/discuss how MacCaig uses metaphor to portray the theme of poverty in his poetry.

N5 This section illustrates how to answer the type of questions asked in the exam. In each case turn to the poem using the page reference given. There are two questions per poem. Each question is followed by some commentary on how to answer the question and then by a possible answer, with the awarding of marks indicated in brackets. The answers are not exhaustive – other answers are also possible.

Assisi (page 6)

1 Look at verse 1.

By referring to two examples of language, explain how the writer creates a contrast in this verse. **4**

Comment

Contrast questions are usually best answered by word choice. Lines 1–4 present the crippled dwarf. Phrases such as 'hands on backwards', 'slumped like a half-filled sack' and 'twisted legs' all present a picture of deformity and ugliness, which contrasts with 'three tiers of churches', 'in honour of St Francis' and 'brother of the poor', which praise and make heroic the saint. The dwarf is ugly and deformed, while St Francis is presented as honourable and of noble stature.

Possible answers

- 'hands on backwards' (1) suggests that the dwarf is crippled (1)
- 'brother of the poor' (1) suggests that St Francis is kind and generous (1)

2 Look at lines 18–20.

By referring to two examples of language, explain how the writer makes clear that the tourists are foolish. **4**

Comment

Again, word choice is perhaps the best way to answer this question. The speaker says that the tourists are 'clucking contentedly', suggesting that they had the intellectual brain power of a hen, and that they 'fluttered' after the priest suggests that they made silly, flapping movements, not at all serious. They followed unthinkingly as the priest scattered the grain of 'the Word', unaware of the starving dwarf outside.

Possible answers

- 'clucking contentedly' (1) suggests that the tourists made child-like noises, acting stupidly, as easily satisfied as a hen (1)
- 'fluttered' (1) suggests that they flocked after the priest mindlessly (1)

Aunt Julia (page 10)

1 Read lines 5–11.

By referring to two examples of contrast, explain how the writer presents the young boy's impression of his aunt. **4**

Comment

To establish contrast, it is best to use word choice. Expressions such as 'She wore men's boots' clearly contrast with 'paddling with the treadle of the spinningwheel', as the former reveals her strength and masculine appearance, while the latter revels her feminine skills. Similarly, 'stained with peat', again suggesting her toughness as she goes barefoot out of doors, contrasts with drawing 'yarn / marvellously out of the air' suggesting that her spinning wheel artistry verges on the magical. Set out the answers clearly:

Possible answers

- 'She wore men's boots' (1) reveals her masculine appearance (1) whereas 'paddling with the treadle of the spinningwheel' (1) reveals her soft, feminine side (1)
- 'stained with peat' (1) suggests her toughness as she goes barefoot out of doors (1), contrasting with drawing 'yarn / marvellously out of the air' (1) suggesting that her spinning wheel artistry verges on the magical (1)

2 Look at lines 17–23.

Explain any two important ideas conveyed in these lines. **2**

Comment

There are a few ideas in these lines: (i) she had to carry water to the croft; (ii) she collected rainwater in buckets; (iii) she was close to nature and the weather; (iv) the weather was often harsh; (v) she was self-sufficient – collected her hens' eggs; (vi) she wore traditional clothes; (vii) she was careful with money.

Possible answers

- the weather where she stayed was often harsh (1)
- she saved money (1)

Basking Shark (page 14)

1 Look at lines 1–3.

Identify two things that we learn about the situation in verse 1.   **2**

Comment

This is an 'identify' question where all you have to do is make two points about the situation in which the speaker finds himself. Underline any two aspects that you can find: for example, we know that he 'stub[s] an oar', which means he is in a rowing boat – there is no need to comment, just state that fact. We know that there is a 'rock where none should be': he knows the sea well. Something emerges out of the sea and scares the speaker.

Possible answers

- the speaker is in a rowing boat on the sea (1)
- he comes across what he thinks is a rock that ought not to be there (1)

2 Look at lines 4–6.

By referring to two examples of language, explain how the writer conveys the change in the speaker's attitude.   **4**

Comment

It is best to answer such a question using word choice. The first indication of a change in his attitude is the use of the conjunction 'But' at the beginning of line 4, introducing the change to 'not too often', a light-hearted remark, qualified by the throwaway phrase after the dash: ' – though enough', which indicates that he doesn't want to repeat the experience. However, it's the expression 'I count as gain' that makes clear his change – now he thinks positively about the experience.

Possible answers

- the use of the conjunction 'But' at the beginning of the verse (1) indicates that his attitude is changing from being nervous about the experience (1)
- 'I count as gain' (1) shows that he now regards the experience as beneficial (1)

Brooklyn Cop (page 18)

1 Read lines 1–5.

By referring to two examples of imagery, explain how the writer creates an impression of the cop. **4**

Comment

To begin with, the speaker compares the cop to a 'gorilla', suggesting his strength and ferocity; 'less timid' suggests that the cop is even more violent and brutal than the gorilla; 'thick-fleshed' suggests that he is animal-like in appearance but suggests also that he is insensitive – as in 'thick-skinned'. The expression 'steak-coloured' is another metaphor comparing his skin colour to that of meat, while further suggesting his animal-like appearance; 'two / hieroglyphs' suggests the scars on his face are to be read with caution.

Possible answers

- 'Built like a gorilla' (1) suggests the cop appears big, strong and brutal (1)
- 'two hieroglyphs' (1) are scars that serve as a warning to others about his viciousness (1)

2 Read lines 17–18.

Explain how these lines make an effective conclusion to the poem. **2**

Comment

Conclusion questions require you to pick an expression from the designated lines and show how it refers back either to an expression or to an idea mentioned earlier or to make some comments about language. The use of 'And' isolates the point being made, and ending the verse and the entire poem with the words 'his victims' concludes the theme of the poem – that violence is a condition of human beings. Even the police can be violent. On this occasion, it is better to base the answer on the use of language.

Possible answers

- beginning the verse with the conjunction 'And' (1) isolates the final point being made, effectively concluding the poem (1)
- ending the verse and the entire poem with the words 'his victims' (1) concludes the theme of the poem – that violence is a condition of human beings. Even the police can be violent and merciless (1)

Hotel Room, 12th Floor (page 22)

1 Read lines 10–11.

By referring to two examples of imagery, explain how the writer creates a sense of danger. **4**

Comment

MacCaig uses the images of 'midnight' and 'defeated' to create the sense of danger. The word 'midnight' is metaphorical, suggesting darkness and evil, while the idea that midnight is 'not / so easily defeated' suggests that evil cannot be overcome without difficulty.

Possible answers

- 'midnight' (1) suggests darkness and, therefore, metaphorically evil (1)
- that midnight is 'not / so easily defeated' (1) suggests that it's difficult to overcome evil (1)

2 Read lines 15–18.

By referring to two examples of language, explain how the writer makes clear the violence on New York's streets. **4**

Comment

The expression 'police cars and ambulances racing' suggests the sheer number of emergencies on the streets. The synecdoche 'broken bones' suggests that there are many injured people to be dealt with; 'harsh screaming' suggests that people are injured or abused, and the enjambement 'blood / glazed on the sidewalks' dramatically separates 'blood' from 'glazed on the sidewalks', forcing it onto a line by itself, highlighting and reinforcing the violent climax to the verse.

Possible answers

- 'police cars and ambulances racing' (1) suggests the sheer number of emergencies on the streets (1)
- 'harsh screaming' (1) suggests that people are being badly injured or abused (1)

Visiting Hour (page 26)

1 Look at lines 31–34.

By referring to two examples of language, show how the writer conveys his feelings at this point in the poem. **4**

Comment

Because this is a language question, you need to think about word choice, imagery and enjambement, among other techniques of language. 'She smiles a little at this': the word 'this' at the end of the line is an intensifier, which, along with the enjambement, highlights 'black figure' at the beginning of the next line. The term 'black figure' could be a reference to the speaker's coat, it could be that she can only see him as a black figure against the whiteness of the hospital or it could be metaphorical, suggesting that it is the figure of death beside her. That he 'clumsily rises' shows his awkwardness as he thinks about her imminent death, but it is the use of synaesthesia – 'round swimming waves of a bell' – where the visual image of 'round swimming waves' is a feature of the sound image of the bell, thereby further capturing his confusion, while 'swimming waves' almost suggests panic on his part at leaving her.

Possible answers

- 'She smiles a little at this': (1) the word 'this', along with the enjambement, highlights 'black figure' at the beginning of the next line, showing that the speaker is thinking about her death (1)

- 'clumsily rises' (1) shows his awkwardness as he thinks about her imminent death (1)

2 Look at lines 35–38.

Using your own words as far as possible, explain **two** important ideas explored in these final lines. **2**

Comment

Because it is a 'use your own words' question, there is no need for quotation/reference, though if you find it easier to answer the question using a reference, there is nothing to stop you – but there are no marks available for this. There are two main ideas explored in these lines: his realisation that she is about to die soon and his sadness at his awareness that he is unlikely to see her again.

Possible answers

- the speaker is confused and sad that his friend is about to die soon (1) and that he is therefore unlikely to see her again (1)

Higher Exam-Style Questions

H This section illustrates how to answer the type of questions asked in the exam. In each case turn to the poem using the page reference given. There are two questions per poem. Each question is followed by some commentary on how to answer the question and then by a possible answer, with the awarding of marks indicated in brackets. The answers are not exhaustive – other answers are also possible.

Assisi (page 6)

1 Look at the opening and closing of the poem.

By referring to at least two examples of contrast, analyse how the writer conveys the hypocrisy of the Church. **2**

Comment

Beginnings and endings of poems often reveal contrast, which is used to reinforce theme. *Assisi* begins with 'The dwarf' and ends with 'St Francis', a contrast that invites the reader to contemplate the difference and similarities between the two men: the one poor, disabled, ugly, the other the saviour of the impoverished. This contrast creates an irony that reveals the hypocrisy of the Church.

Possible answers

- the poem begins with the words 'The dwarf' and ends with 'St Francis', creating between the two men a contrast that helps reveal the theme of hypocrisy of a church that ignores the former and celebrates the latter (2)

2 Read lines 1–9.

By referring to at least two examples of contrast, analyse how the writer presents the dwarf and St Francis. **4**

Comment

The expression 'hands on backwards' conveys the extent of the dwarf's appalling deformities, while the simile 'half-filled sack' not only recalls the hessian that used to be worn by monks but also suggests by 'half-filled' and 'slumped' that he cannot support himself; 'twisted legs from which / sawdust might run' suggests that his legs are wooden with sawdust pouring from them, which is a shocking image recalling a scarecrow, linking to the other references to birds. St Francis is presented as someone who talks with birds, not someone who scares them. St Francis is also presented as a 'brother / of the poor', a hugely ironic statement, given the poor person beside the church. The expression 'brother / of the poor' suggests that St Francis chose to live as a beggar (we know that was the case), while the dwarf has no choice.

- 'hands on backwards' conveys the extent of the dwarf's appalling deformities; the simile 'half-filled sack' not only recalls the hessian that used to be worn by monks but also suggests by 'half-filled' and 'slumped' that the dwarf cannot support himself (2)
- 'brother of the poor' suggests that St Francis chose to live as a beggar, while the dwarf has no choice because the Church neglects him, thus establishing the irony of the situation and the hypocrisy of the Church (2)

Aunt Julia (page 10)

1 Look at lines 5–16.

By referring to at least two examples of language, analyse how the poet makes clear everything Aunt Julia signifies. **4**

Comment

You can choose to answer the question using four examples, with basic comments, each worth 1 mark, or you can use two examples, each with a more detailed comment worth 2 marks (that is, 1 + 1 + 1 + 1 or 1 + 1 + 2 or 2 + 2). You must give a reference but it is not worth any marks.

Several references signify what the speaker's aunt represents for him: for example, 'men's boots' suggests that she appears to him strong and manly in appearance; 'when she wore any' suggests that she was tough and resilient, used to harsh conditions. Her 'strong foot' signifies her sheer physical vigour; 'stained with peat' indicates she has to fetch fuel, working hard to do so. On the other hand, 'paddling with … while her right hand' suggests that she can perform tasks traditionally associated with women, skilfully and dexterously. The word 'marvellously' suggests his awe, she reminds him of fairy tales. The expression 'Hers was the only house' indicates that there was nowhere else like it and he felt safe there, while 'crickets being friendly' suggests he felt relaxed and happy there.

Possible answers

- 'men's boots' signifies a masculine side to her character; the fact that sometimes she wore no boots indicates that she was remarkably tough and resilient, used to harsh conditions (2)
- her 'strong foot' signifies her sheer physical vigour (1)
- 'stained with peat' indicates that she is more involved with work than appearances (1)

2 Look at verse 5.

By referring to at least two examples, analyse how the writer's use of language suggests the speaker's regrets. **4**

Comment

Lines 24–36 recall the opening lines 1–4. In line 26, 'By the time' indicates that something has happened, that the young boy is now an adult. However, 'by the time I had learned / a little' Gaelic, Aunt Julia already 'lay / silenced' – she was already dead and that caused him regret as she had been a very vocal, quick talker, but now can't speak; 'the absolute black' of 'a sandy grave' suggests the finality of death, with 'black' conveying his despairing attitude to death. That he can 'hear her still' is all in his imagination (as he doesn't believe in any afterlife), while the final three lines express his anger and regret that they never had the conversation that they should have had while she was still alive.

Possible answers

- 'By the time I had learned' signals that time has passed and something of significance has happened – the young boy has become a man, but Aunt Julia is now dead and he so regrets that (2)

- the idea that she 'lay / silenced' is also cause for regret as she was a very vocal, quick talker, but now can't speak because she is dead (1)

- the final three lines – the repetition of 'getting angry, getting angry' – expresses his anger and regret that they never had the conversation that they should have had while she was still alive (1)

Basking Shark (page 14)

1 Read lines 1–3.

Analyse how effective these lines are as an opening to the poem. **2**

Comment

Lines 1–3 introduce the subject matter. 'To stub an oar' makes clear that he is in a rowing boat; 'on a rock where none should be' reveals that he has hit something that should not be there; 'slounge out of the sea' – the object actually moves and has risen out of the sea; 'once (too often) to me' indicates that he does not want to repeat the experience.

Possible answers

- 'To stub an oar' – he is in a rowing boat and 'on a rock where none should be' suggests he has come across something that shouldn't be there (1)

- 'once (too often) to me' indicates by the parenthetical '(too often)' that he does not want to repeat the experience (1)

2   Read lines 13–15.

By referring to the poet's use of language, evaluate the effectiveness of these lines as a conclusion to the poem.   **2**

Comment

The rhetorical question (one that implies its own answer) effectively ends the poem, underlining the point that the speaker has changed his mind about the shark – it is not the monster he thought it was in line 6. Now he realises, but doesn't state explicitly, that humans are the monster. His description of the gracefully departing shark conveys his respect for it. The long 'a' vowel sound of the internal rhymes – 'pale', 'sail after sail' and 'tail' – convey the elegant beauty of the shark, comparing it to a ship departing.

Possible answers

- the rhetorical question underlines the point that the speaker has changed his mind about the shark – it is not the monster he thought it was in line 6; now he realises that humans are the monster (1)

- the use of the agreeable long 'a' vowel sound supports the point that the shark is leaving him elegantly (1)

Brooklyn Cop (page 18)

1   Look at lines 1–9.

By referring to at least two examples, analyse how the poet's use of language creates an impression of the cop.   **4**

Comment

The simile in line 1 – 'Built like a gorilla' – immediately establishes the cop as powerful and brutal; 'but less timid' suggests that he is even more vicious than the comparison suggests. The compound adjectives are used metaphorically to present the cop, with 'thick-fleshed' suggesting that he is animal-like in appearance; 'thick' implies that he appears to lack intelligence; 'steak-coloured' suggests his tanned skin colour and his toughness. The metaphor 'two hieroglyphs' compares his scars to ancient symbols, which, deciphered, spell out danger. The metaphor 'thin tissue over violence' portrays the veneer of civilisation as flimsily thin – all that protects us from violence. The contrast between his routine departing cliché – '"See you, babe"' – and his evening greeting – '"Hiya, honey" is no cliché' – makes clear his relief at having got home safely. In line 8, the simile in the opening line has changed to a metaphor – 'He is a gorilla': the use of **zoomorphism** portraying him as a fierce aggressor.

Possible answers

- the simile in line 1 – 'Built like a gorilla' – immediately establishes the cop as powerful and brutal; 'but less timid' suggests that he is even more vicious than the comparison suggests (2)

- the contrast between his routine departing clichéd '"See you, babe"' and his evening greeting '"Hiya, honey" is no cliché' makes clear his relief at having got home safely (2)

- in line 8, the simile of the opening line has changed to a metaphor – 'He is a gorilla': the use of zoomorphism portraying him as a fierce aggressor (2)

2 Read lines 14–18.

By referring to the poet's use of language, evaluate the effectiveness of these lines as a conclusion to the poem.   **2**

Comment

MacCaig uses two rhetorical questions in these final two sentences. Rhetorical questions are used to make a point, usually to invite the reader to agree with the writer: in the case of the penultimate verse, the speaker asks who would want to be the cop, given the horrors of his job. The use of zoomorphism once more compares him to a gorilla, this time with a police baton, ready for use. The parenthetical ', this time,' delays the climactic 'never get back to', creating some sympathy for the cop. Lines 17–18 are complicated, because although they still use a rhetorical question, the lines begin with the conjunction 'And', which has the effect of highlighting the very last point by isolating it. The repetition of 'who' in 'who would be' and 'who have to be' draws attention to the complexity of the question – the reader has to take time to work out that the speaker is finally making the point that the cop has 'victims', thereby subverting his role as a policeman. He is no different from the violent criminals he is supposed to protect people from. Any sympathy established for him in the penultimate verse is undermined by the final comment that his methods are no better than the violent, vicious criminals he is supposed to protect people from. The final verse establishes the deep irony surrounding the Brooklyn Cop.

Possible answers

- the penultimate and final verses form the conclusion by their use of two rhetorical questions: the first in the penultimate verse engages sympathy for the cop by the use of climax, delaying the point that he may 'never get back to' his home – no-one would want to be in that position. In the final verse, however, he subverts the cop's role by portraying him as having 'victims' as well as the criminals (2)

Hotel Room, 12th Floor (page 22)

1 Read lines 1–5.

By referring to at least two examples of language, analyse how the writer conveys the speaker's attitude to New York. **4**

Comment

The simile, 'a helicopter skirting like a damaged insect', compares the symbol of modern technology (the context is the 1960s) to a 'damaged insect', suggesting not only the fragility of the aircraft but also the difficulty nature has of surviving in an unnatural urban environment. The comparison of the scale of the 'insect' against the Empire State Building emphasises how huge this tallest of buildings (at the time) appeared. To compare the building to a 'jumbo size dentist's drill' again suggests the size of the building, but also, because dentist's drills suggest pain, the image conveys agonising distress. The personification in 'landing / on the roof of the PanAm skyscraper' continues the idea of the insect, where 'skyscraper' has a pejorative, dismissive tone.

Possible answers

- the simile – 'a helicopter skirting like a damaged insect' – compares the symbol of modern technology to a 'damaged insect', suggesting not only the fragility of the aircraft but also the difficulty that nature has to survive in such an unnatural urban environment (2)

- the metaphor – 'jumbo size dentist's drill' – suggests the sheer size of the building as well as suggesting pain – he regards all that he is witnessing as agonisingly distressing (2)

2 Read lines 11–14 (from 'I lie in bed' to 'canyons and gulches').

Analyse how the poet uses language to convey his concerns at this point in the poem. **2**

Comment

That he lies 'in bed, between / a radio and a television set' suggests that he is trying to drown out the noise of the city around and below him. The caesura after 'set' forces 'the wildest of warwhoops continually ululating through' into the next line, thereby shocking the reader – the sudden transition to Wild West imagery is incongruous to the urban setting. The expression 'the glittering canyons and gulches' develops the Wild West theme and shows that the noise and violence isn't new but is a progression from a previous era in America. The onomatopoeic 'ululating' is blood-curdling, portraying his concern about the shocking violence. The alliteration of the hard gutturals in 'glittering canyons and gulches' draws attention to the harshness of the environment.

Possible answers

- that he lies 'in bed, between / a radio and a television set' suggests that he is trying to drown out the noise of the city around and below him (1)

- the caesura after 'set' forces 'the wildest of warwhoops continually ululating through' into the next line, surprising and shocking the reader by the sudden transition to Wild West imagery that is incongruous to the urban setting (2)

- the onomatopoeic 'ululating' is almost blood-curdling, portraying his concern about the shocking violence (1)

Visiting Hour (page 26)

1 Look at lines 1–7.

By referring to at least two examples, explain/analyse how MacCaig uses language to convey a light-hearted tone. **2**

Comment

In *Visiting Hour*, though a very serious poem, there are attempts by the speaker to try and lighten the tone as a means of coping with his distraught feelings. The idea that the 'hospital smell / combs [his] nostrils' is amusing in its use of personification (how can a hospital smell comb nostrils?) and the very oddity of the image (combing nostrils) draws attention to the overwhelming smell of hospitals, suggesting that it attacks our sense of smell – the image is amusing in its ability to surprise. The image of his nostrils 'bobbing along' the corridor is also amusing in that he suggests his nose has a life of its own. The image of the corpse being 'trundled into a lift' and vanishing 'heavenward' is also amusing because, as a professed atheist, MacCaig did not believe in heaven or any afterlife. In the last line of verse 2, the one word 'heavenward' is ironic.

Possible answers

- 'bobbing along' suggests that his nostrils have a life of their own, a synecdochic image, where the nostrils represent himself but at the same time draw attention to the fact that the hospital smell blocks out all his senses except his nose; also, the word 'bobbing' connotes an amusing up and down, almost jaunty movement, that effectively lightens the mood, a way of coping with his feelings (2)

2 Look at lines 11–18.

By referring to at least two examples, analyse how MacCaig uses language to convey the speaker's anxiety. **4**

Comment

His anxiety is communicated by comparing himself to the nurses; he observes the nurses as they walk 'lightly, swiftly', both adverbs modifying the verb 'walk', suggesting that their walk is unexacting and effortless, almost casual, a contrast with his feelings of apprehension, confusion and inadequacy (contrast being a feature of language). The normal word order of 'here and there and up and down' has been inverted, placing 'there' right at the end of the line, thus capturing the nurses' **ubiquitous** (everywhere at once) presence and ability to multi-task. The use of polysyndeton (repetition of the conjunction between each item) adds to the pace and their confidence; 'their slender waists' contrasts with how they can carry the painful 'burden', highlighting and contrasting with his inability to deal with the situation. The anaphora (the repetition of 'so much/so many') emphasises his admiration of their ability to deal with death and dying. The enjambement in 'their eyes / still clear' draws attention to 'still clear', revealing his respect for the way they cope unemotionally with death – whereas he is full of confusion and apprehension.

Possible answers

- his observation that the nurses walk 'lightly, swiftly' indicates that their manner seems quick and effortless, almost casual, contrasting with his feelings of apprehension and lack of certainty; by contrast, he feels inadequate (2)

- the speaker's use of anaphora – 'so much/so many' – emphasises his understanding and admiration of their ability to deal with death and dying (1)

- the enjambement 'their eyes / still clear' draws attention to 'still clear', again revealing his admiration that they can cope unemotionally with their dying patients, whereas he is full of confusion and apprehension (1)

Basking Shark

To stub an oar on a rock where none should be,
To have it rise with a slounge out of the sea
Is a thing that happened once (too often) to me.

But not too often – though enough. I count as gain
5 That once I met, on a sea tin-tacked with rain,
That roomsized monster with a matchbox brain.

He displaced more than water. He shoggled me
Centuries back – this decadent townee
Shook on a wrong branch of his family tree.

10 Swish up the dirt and, when it settles, a spring
Is all the clearer. I saw me, in one fling,
Emerging from the slime of everything.

So who's the monster? The thought made me grow pale
For twenty seconds while, sail after sail,
15 The tall fin slid away and then the tail.

N5 Questions

1. Look at lines 1–3.
    Identify, in the first three lines of the poem, two main ideas of the poem.　2

2. Look at lines 3–6.
    Show how two examples of the writer's use of language suggest the
    speaker's feelings at this stage in the poem.　4

3. Look at lines 10–12.
    Explain how the writer's use of metaphor clarifies his thinking.　4

4. Look at lines 13–15.
    How effective do you find these lines as a conclusion to the poem?　2

5. By referring to this poem and at least one other by MacCaig, show how
    the poet uses nature as a feature of his poetry.　8

H Questions

1. Look at lines 1–3.
    Analyse how language is used to convey the speaker's feelings.　2

2. Look at lines 7–12.
    By referring to at least two examples, analyse how the use of poetic
    technique clarifies the speaker's thinking.　4

3. Look at lines 13–15.
    By referring to at least two examples, analyse how language is used to
    reveal that the speaker has changed his mind.　4

4. By referring to this poem and at least one other by MacCaig, show how
    the poet uses sound to convey the ideas in his poetry.　10

Glossary

Adjective – a word that describes a noun.

Adverb – a word or phrase that modifies a verb, another adverb or a sentence, for example, slowly, easily, cleverly.

Alliteration/alliterative – repetition of the same consonants, usually to highlight what is being said.

Anaphora – the repetition of a word or phrase at the beginning of a sentence or a series of sentences.

Assonance – repetition of similar vowel sounds to create rhyme or to highlight (usually the tone) what is being said.

Asyndetic – describes a list with no conjunctions between items.

Caesura – a gap near the middle of a line of poetry, usually created by the use of a punctuation mark.

Cliché – an overused expression, lacking in originality.

Climax – a significant or dramatic final point.

Collective noun – a singular noun that refers to a group of people or animals (a *pride* of lions).

Complement – the object of a sentence; in 'The boy crossed the road' the complement or object is 'the road'.

Compound adjective – an adjective formed by the combination of two separate words (thick-fleshed).

Connotation – whatever a word suggests (rather than means).

Connote – suggest.

Contrast – two ideas, words or images that appear opposite or very different but which together reveal an underlying significance.

Declarative (sentence) – a sentence which makes an assertion or gives information in a definite way.

End-stopped (line) – the natural break at the end of a line of poetry, created usually by a punctuation mark.

Enjambement – when sentence structure takes priority over line structure.

First-person narration – where a character or speaker uses 'I' or 'me'.

Free verse – verse which has no regular rhythm or rhyme.

Fresco – a plastered wall that has been painted on while the plaster is still wet.

Fricative – the 'f' sound.

Frugality – thrifty, careful with money.

Giotto – an artist from Florence (b.1267–d.1337), most famous for his development of naturalistic painting.

Guttural – sound made at the back of the throat.

Hyperbole – the use of exaggeration for heightened effect.

Image/imagery – mental picture of an idea or object.

Infinitive – the basic form of a verb following 'to', without a particular subject or tense (to be, to have, to run).

Intensifier – word which increases the strength of an adjective or adverb term (very, extremely).

Irony – stating the opposite of what is meant in order to make a significant point.

Juxtaposition – the placing of words, images or ideas side by side.

Kinetic (energy) – describing anything in terms of movement.

Line break – a deliberate break at the end of a line, forcing the sentence to spill over onto the next line, drawing attention to the beginning of the next line.

List – series of items usually separated by commas or by conjunctions.

Literal – the explicit meaning of a word.

Metaphor – a device of comparison, saying one thing is something else.

Minor (one-word) sentence – a sentence without a main verb.

Onomatopoeia – using a word which sounds the same as the sound of the thing it names.

Oxymoron – words or ideas that appear to be contradictions.

Paradox – words, phrases, images or ideas that seem to contradict each other.

Parenthetical/parentheses – an expression that is additional to a sentence yet grammatically independent, usually signalled by pairs of brackets or dashes but sometimes commas.

Pejorative – the tone of a word that suggests disapproval or unpleasantness.

Penultimate – second last item in a series of items.

Persona – the speaker in a poem.

Personification – ascribing human qualities to inanimate objects.

Plosive – the hard 'b' and 'p' sounds.

Polysyndeton – the placing of conjunctions (and, or, nor, if) between each item in a list to intensify the point being made.

Relative pronouns – who, which, that, whose.

Repetition – words, phrases or expressions repeated for emphasis or dramatic effect. The repetition of phrases at the beginning of sentences or clauses is called *anaphora*.

Rhetorical question – a question that implies its own answer.

Rhyme – words with the same or similar vowel sounds, often at the end of lines of poetry (spring, fling).

Rhyme scheme – the pattern of sounds used at the end of lines of poetry, usually indicated by lower case letters (e.g. *a a b b* or *a b b a*).

Rhythm – a repeated pattern of stressed sound, although the repetition does not have to be regular.

Sarcastic – stating the opposite of what is meant in order to ridicule or mock.

Sibilant – the soft 's' and 'z' sounds, creating a hissing sound.

Simile – a device of comparison, saying one thing is like something else.

Sound image – a mental representation of a sound.

Stereotype – a fixed or simplified idea about what someone or something is like using a set of characteristics (accent, dress, hair style).

Symbolism/symbol – the use of an object, place or person to represent something else.

Synaesthesia – one sense being perceived as another.

Synecdoche – where a part of something is used to represent the whole.

Tense – the use of verbs to indicate time (present – *I jump*; past – *I jumped*; future – *I shall jump*).

Tension – usually associated with the build up of stress or suspense.

Third-person (narration) – where the reader is addressed by someone not part of the narrative, using 'he', 'she' or 'they'.

Tone – the feeling of a piece of writing that conveys the writer's attitude to the subject matter.

Transferred epithet – where an adjective associated with a person is used to describe an inanimate object.

Ubiquitous – everywhere and ever present.

Verse paragraph – where one verse leads on from the previous verse while exploring a different aspect of content.

Word choice – a word or words used for their connotative meaning and effect.

Zoomorphism – the attribution of animal characteristics to humans.

Answers

Note that the following answers are not exhaustive; they show possible answers and indicate the allocation of marks (e.g. (1)).

Pages 6–9, *Assisi*

N5
- 'hands on backwards' (1) suggests that the dwarf is badly deformed or else his hands are facing upwards, begging for money (1)
- 'tiny twisted legs' (1) emphasises how small he is and that his legs are severely deformed (1)

H
- by the use of the simile 'half-filled sack' MacCaig reminds us of the hessian that used to be worn by monks, thereby recalling the connection with St Francis, but also 'half-filled' suggests just how slight he is, and 'slumped' highlights the fact that he cannot support himself (2)
- the alliteration of the 't' sound in 'tiny twisted' reinforces the whole image – 'tiny twisted legs', reinforcing how crippled he is, and the enjambement in lines 3–4 highlights the word 'sawdust', suggesting how insubstantial and weak his legs are (2)

Pages 10–13, *Aunt Julia*

N5
- 'She wore men's boots' (1) suggests that he was small enough in height to notice the kind of footwear she wore (1)
- 'marvellously' (1) suggests that because he was so young, her actions seemed almost magical to him (1)

H
- the word choice 'I can see her strong foot' suggests that he was so small at the time that he could notice her feet, and the use of the word 'strong' makes clear that he was young enough to be impressed by the power in her feet as she went barefoot (2)
- the contrast between 'men's boots' and 'strong foot' on the one hand and 'paddling with the treadle of the spinningwheel' impresses him because the contrast between her masculine appearance and her feminine domesticity is something only a young child would note (2)

- the word 'marvellously' highlights his fascination and amazement, as her skills seem to him almost unbelievable (1)

Pages 14–17, *Basking Shark*

N5
- the question 'So who's the monster?' (1) recalls line 6 – 'That roomsized monster' (1)
- 'and then the tail' (1) suggests the end of the poem with the word 'tail', the end part of the shark (1)

H
- the use of repetition of 'sail' as well as the internal rhyme, along with the alliteration of the 's' and 't' sounds, all draw attention to the slow movement of the shark away from the poet, thus concluding the poem (2)

Pages 18–21, *Brooklyn Cop*

N5
- 'what clubbings' (1) suggests that he could easily be the badly beaten-up victim of criminals (1)
- the name 'Whamburger' (1) connotes violence, especially with the first syllable 'Wham' (1)

H
- the rhetorical question 'Who would be him?' has the implied answer of not the reader, his life is too dangerous (1)
- 'what clubbings' suggests that he could easily be the badly beaten-up victim of criminals (1)
- 'gunshots', with assonance of the guttural short 'u' sound, is a violent, ugly word, connoting injuring or even death (1)
- the name 'Whamburger' connotes violence, especially with the onomatopoeic first syllable 'Wham', suggesting a sudden and violent action (1)

Pages 22–25, *Hotel Room, 12th Floor*

N5
- 'uncivilised' (1) connotes barbarous, primitive behaviour (1)
- 'darkness' (1) suggests evil by the image of 'darkness', which has connotations of threat and wickedness (1)

H
- the enjambement 'darkness / is shot at by a million lit windows' draws attention to the contrast between darkness (evil) and light (good), but the use of the expression 'shot at' suggests that although the 'lit windows' are trying to destroy the darkness, they do so violently ('shot') (2)

74 Answers

- the upper-case 'M' on 'Midnight', along with the use of personification ('Midnight has come in') has the effect of suggesting midnight has a mind of its own and will come in despite our efforts; resistance is useless (2)

Pages 26–29, *Visiting Hour*

N5 • 'black figure' (1) suggests he is alive (1), his appearance contrasting with her 'white' (1) appearance, 'white' signifying her illness and nearness to death (1)

- the oxymoron 'fruitless fruits' (1) is in itself a contrast portraying his despair – 'fruits' are health-giving, yet they are fruitless because there is no point in giving them to her as she will die soon; the image reflects his upset (1)

H • by his use of colour: the speaker contrasts his 'black figure' with his friend in her 'white cave', thereby suggesting that he appears to be in despair (connotations of 'black') while 'white cave' suggests that she is surrounded by illness – 'white' connoting illness – deathly white, for example; the speaker's despair and fear concerning the imminent death of his friend are represented by the symbol of the grim reaper suggested by the word 'black' (2)

- the oxymoron 'fruitless fruits' reveals contrast through the apparent contradiction: 'fruit' is a traditional, healthy gift for hospital patients from loved ones, but here 'fruit' is qualified by the adjective 'fruitless', suggesting the pointlessness of such a gift; the apparent contradiction portrays his despondency and fear (2)

- there is also the suggestion that his visit (symbolised by 'fruit') is 'fruitless', given her forgetfulness, illness and nearness to death, thus his despair and fears (1)

Pages 32–33, Isolation 1

Assisi

- in *Assisi*, MacCaig reveals the isolation of the dwarf by placing him outside the three tiers of churches – the tourists ignore him because they are too preoccupied with the priest and his explanation of Giotto's frescoes

- he is also isolated from St Francis, the 'brother / of the poor' and therefore the symbol of goodness and support; everyone 'had passed / the ruined temple outside' – and the word 'outside' indicates his isolation

Pages 34–35, Isolation 2

Aunt Julia

- Aunt Julia represents a traditional, but disappearing Scottish way of life, and her – and therefore its – isolation is highlighted by the fact that she spoke Gaelic, but the speaker couldn't – he was unable to understand her questions

- Aunt Julia's isolation is complete when she is 'in the absolute black / of a sandy grave'

Visiting Hour

- the isolation of the speaker's ill friend is emphasised in the fifth verse: he states that 'she lies / in a white cave of forgetfulness' suggesting that, because of her illness, she cannot remember who he is, and he sees her in a cave, isolated from everybody

- the greatest isolation that is expressed is when he 'goes off, growing fainter, / not smaller' – from the patient's perspective he seems faint, out of focus, but from his own perspective he isn't any smaller in stature; he feels isolated by her imminent death

Pages 36–37, Nature

Basking Shark

- the poem is all about nature – both animal and human; his use of rhyming triplets throughout the poem gives the poem a very tight feel, in keeping with the intensity of the speaker's thinking throughout, which is about his shift from regarding the shark as monster to regarding the human beings as monstrous. That shift occurs over a few verses and the use of rhyming triplets helps the reader follow the process

Hotel Room, 12th Floor

- this poem also deals with the effects of human nature – not only what humans do to each other, but the underlying cruelty that is part of what it is to be human; human society is unequal and poverty is portrayed by the gap conveyed by the symbols of power and wealth on the one hand and on the other hand the poor, destined to live in 'coldwater flats' – the most destitute of living conditions for New York's underprivileged

Answers

- the 'blood / glazed on the sidewalks' also symbolises the cruelty and violence that are both an integral part of what it is to be human

Pages 38–39, Dark Side of Human Nature

Brooklyn Cop

- *Brooklyn Cop* is essentially all about human nature: the suggestion is that the police have to be like gorillas – large, strong, aggressive – in order to survive on the streets of New York; the cop – symbol of the police force – faces 'clubbings', 'gunshots' – symbols of violence – every day

- the most depressing comment that MacCaig makes, though, is that the cop makes the criminals 'victims', suggesting that he is no different from the people he is supposed to be protecting society from – cruelty and violence are an endemic part of human nature

Pages 42–43, Sound Effects

Assisi

- The dwarf with his hands on backwards sat, slumped like a half-filled sack

  In these lines, the alliteration of the sibilant (the 's' sound) makes an unpleasant hissing noise, which highlights the repulsive appearance of the dwarf, who cannot even sit properly

Pages 44–45, Enjambement

Aunt Julia

- by the use of the caesura in 'and getting angry, getting angry', the speaker forces 'with so many questions' onto the next line, thereby drawing attention to its meaning – that these questions haven't gone away, a thought clarified by forcing the final word 'unanswered' onto the final line of the poem, revealing his frustration and annoyance that so much was left unsaid and unresolved at the death of his aunt

Pages 46–47, Comparison

Basking Shark

- 'Swish up the dirt' is both literal (the shark disturbed the sediment by its movement) and metaphorical (the appearance of the shark to the speaker disturbed his previous thinking about the primitive nature of the shark)

- 'Shook on the wrong branch of his family tree' is a metaphor suggesting that human beings (species also known as *Homo sapiens*) have developed in a wrong direction on the tree of life, and are now in a precarious position

Pages 48–49, Representation and Contrast

Hotel Room, 12th Floor

- in the first verse, contrast is used to establish the shift in time: 'This morning' establishes that the speaker is referring to his experiences earlier in the day (note the past tense), whereas 'Midnight' (line 6) establishes the shift to present time, reinforced by the conjunction 'But' and by the use of the present tense

- contrast is used not only to establish the shift in time, but to highlight the shift from descriptive appearances, however unpleasant (lines 1–5), to the more sinister idea of threat (lines 6–9), especially the threat from 'foreign places' and of 'uncivilised darkness'

Pages 50–51, Rhythm and Sentence Structure

Brooklyn Cop

- the final sentence is in the form of a rhetorical question, implying that no-one would want to be his victim

- but more than that, the complex sentence structure – with its rhythmic repetiton of 'who would be' and 'who have to be' – makes the reader think twice to get at the meaning – that no-one would want to be those who have to be his victims, and it's the 'who have to be' that makes us realise that they have no choice but to be at the receiving end of his violence, but the use of 'victims', as the last climatic word, makes clear that they are prey to his evil, unlawful behaviour

N5 1
- the speaker is out on the sea in a rowing boat (1)
- his oar hits an unexpected object (1)

2
- 'is a thing' (1) suggests that he is unable to identify what his oar has struck (1)
- 'happened once (too often)' (1) suggests that he is shaken by the experience and doesn't want it repeated (1)

3
- the metaphor 'Swish up the dirt' (1) compares the disturbance of the mud by the shark to the disturbance of his thinking (1)
- 'a spring / Is all the clearer' (1) compares the idea of a spring of water to the clear thoughts he now has (1)
- 'in one fling' (1) compares the idea of sudden forceful movement to the speed with which he realises that all animals emerge from the same origin (1)

4
- the final reference to the shark leaving 'then the tail' (1) recalls the title of the poem (1)

5 *Commonality*
- *Basking Shark* deals with the change in the speaker's thinking from seeing the shark as a monster to realising that human beings are the monster and therefore should not feel superior. On the other hand, in *Hotel Room, 12th Floor* MacCaig realises that an urban environment causes difficulties for nature to survive (2)

Given poem
- in *Basking Shark*, MacCaig in line 6 refers to the monster as huge ('roomsized monster') but stupid ('with a matchbox brain') (1) but by line 13 he suggests by the use of the rhetorical question that the shark isn't the monster, it is human beings who are monstrous (1)

Hotel Room, 12th Floor
- the simile 'like a damaged insect' (1) suggests that insects can find survival difficult in New York (1). He uses the natural environment – 'canyons and gulches' (1) – to compare New York streets to the physical environment of the Wild West, to show that violence occurred in the natural environment just as it does in an urban environment (1)

H 1
- the use of the word choice 'stub' suggests that his oar struck the object with such force that it surprised the speaker (1)
- 'where none should be' makes clear that he didn't expect the object to be there and that made him nervous (1)

2
- the metaphor 'He displaced more than water' compares the shark's physical dislodgement of water because of his bulk to the dislodgement of the speaker's received ideas about small-brained creatures, which leads him to reconsider his views about evolutionary progression (2)
- he uses the metaphor 'Emerging from the slime of everything' to convey his realisation that all creatures – the shark and human beings – originated from the same source; the word 'slime', however, perhaps suggests that the origin of life was not at all glamorous and that human beings shouldn't think themselves superior (2)

3
- the rhetorical question – 'So who's the monster?' – underlines his change of mind: the question implies the answer that human beings are the monster. 'The thought made me grow pale' suggests that this change in his thinking about the nature of evolution disturbs him significantly as he has to adjust to his rejection of received ideas about the relationship between animals and humans (2)
- the use of the internal rhymes 'pale', 'sail after sail' and 'tail', with their use of the long pleasant 'a' sounds, creates an image of the shark as elegant, graceful and beautiful, which so contrasts with his earlier depiction of the shark that we realise that he has now changed his mind about the creature (2)

4 *Commonality*
- both *Basking Shark* and *Visiting Hour* use sound devices to convey the themes of the poems. *Basking Shark* uses rhyming triplets to create a condensed feel, which reflects the intensity and comprehensiveness of the speaker's thinking. In *Visiting Hour*, he uses sound to convey the speaker's apprehension and confusion, as well as the upset he feels when he sees his friend so near to death (2)

Answers

Given poem

- the rhyming triplets use pure vowel sounds and pure rhymes, which help to give the poem its intensity. The speaker also uses onomatopoeia: words such as 'stub' and 'swish' help create the sounds of the sea and therefore add to the atmosphere – and perceived danger – of the encounter with the shark. The assonance of the long 'a' sound in the last three lines creates a pleasant, graceful image of the shark in the water (2)

Visiting Hour

- in *Visiting Hour*, MacCaig uses several sound devices to help portray the theme of the poem – isolation and death. In line 3, for example, he talks about his nostrils 'bobbing' as he walks along the corridor: the word is onomatopoeic, which along with the alliteration of the plosive 'b' sound, create a jolly, jaunty sound to disguise his mood of apprehension and trepidation (2)

- rhythm is a way of capturing the sound of everyday speech and MacCaig uses rhythm to capture sound in 'I will not feel, I will not / feel, until / I have to': the repetition of 'I will not feel' creates a rhythm, which along with the enjambment, creates pauses and stresses that capture speech, emphasising that he must postpone his feelings of dread until he sees his friend (2)

- the use of alliteration in 'wasted / of colour a glass fang is fixed, / not guzzling but giving': the guttural hard 'c' and 'g' sounds create a hard, unpleasant sound that echoes his shock at what he sees. The sounds also replicate the harshness of the subverted vampiric image. The alliteration of the fricative 'f' sound, also unpleasant, especially when used with short vowel sounds of 'fang' and 'fixed', also create unpleasant sounds that resonate with the reader's experiences of hospital visiting (2)